BEETHOVEN

BIOGRAPHIES
AND APPRECIATIONS

By

VARIOUS

Read & Co.

Copyright © 2020 Read & Co. Books

This edition is published by Read & Co. Books,
an imprint of Read & Co.

This book is copyright and may not be reproduced or copied in any
way without the express permission of the publisher in writing.

British Library Cataloguing-in-Publication Data
A catalogue record for this book is available
from the British Library.

Read & Co. is part of Read Books Ltd.
For more information visit
www.readandcobooks.co.uk

CONTENTS

_____

3

ILLUSTRATIONS

BEETHOVEN

BIOGRAPHIES
AND APPRIECIATIONS

BEETHOVEN

By Maurice Baring

More mighty than the hosts of mortal kings,
I hear the legions gathering to their goal;
The tramping millions drifting from one pole,
The march, the counter-march, the flank that swings.
I hear the beating of tremendous wings,
The shock of battle and the drums that roll;
And far away the solemn belfries toll,
And in the field the careless shepherd sings.

There is an end unto the longest day.
The echoes of the fighting die away.
The evening breathes a benediction mild.
The sunset fades. There is no need to weep,
For night has come, and with the night is sleep,
And now the fiercest foes are reconciled.

A POEM FROM
Poems, 1914-1919

7

LUDWIG VAN BEETHOVEN

By Elbert Hubbard

Melody has by Beethoven been freed from the influence of Fashion and changing Taste, and raised to an ever-valid, purely human type. Beethoven's music will be understood to all time, while that of his predecessors will, for the most part, only remain intelligible to us through the medium of reflection on the history of Art.

—RICHARD WAGNER

Music is the youngest of the arts. Modern music dates back about four hundred years. It is not so old as the invention of printing. As an art it began with the work of the priests of the Roman Catholic Church in endeavoring to arrange a liturgy.

The medieval chant and the popular folk-song came together, and the science of music was born. Sculpture reached perfection in Greece, painting in Italy, portraiture in Holland; but Germany, the land of thought, has given us nearly all the great musicians and nine-tenths of all our valuable musical compositions.

Holland has taken a very important part in every line of art and handicraft, and in way of all-round development has set the pace for civilization.

Art follows in the wake of commerce, for without commerce there is neither surplus wealth nor leisure. The artist is paid from what is left after men have bought food and clothing; and the time to enjoy comes only after the struggle for existence.

When Venice was not only Queen of the Adriatic but of the maritime world as well, Art came and established there her Court of Beauty. It was Venice that mothered Giorgione, Titian, the Bellinis, and the men who wrought in iron and silver and gold, and those masterful bookmakers; it was beautiful Venice that gave sustenance and encouragement to Stradivari (who made violins as well as he could) up at Cremona, only a few miles away.

But there came a day when all those seventy bookmakers of Venice ceased to print, and the music of the anvils was stilled, and all the painters were dead, and Venice became but a monument of things that were, as she is today; for Commerce is King, and his capital has been moved far away.

So Venice sits sad and solitary—a pale and beautiful ruin, pathetic beyond speech, infested by noisy shop-keepers and petty pilferers, the degenerate sons of the robbers who once roamed the sea and enthroned her on her hundred isles.

All that Venice knew was absorbed by Holland. The Elzevirs and the Plantins took over the business of the seventy bookmakers, and the art-schools of Amsterdam, Leyden and Antwerp reproduced every picture of note that had been done in Venice. The great churches of Holland are replicas of the churches of Venice. And the Cathedral at Antwerp, where the sweet bells have chimed each quarter of an hour for three centuries, through peace and plenty, through lurid war and sudden death—there where hangs Rubens' masterpiece—that Cathedral is but an enlarged "Santa Maria de' Frari," where for two hundred years hung "The Assumption," by Titian.

In these churches of Holland were placed splendid organs, and the priests formed choirs, and offered prizes for the best singing and the best compositions. Music and painting developed hand in hand; for at the last, all of the arts are one—each being but a division of labor.

The world owes a great debt to the Dutch. It was Holland taught England how to paint and how to print, and England taught us: so our knowledge of printing and painting came to us by way of the apostolic succession of the Dutch.

The march of civilization follows a simple trail, well defined beyond dispute. Viewed in retrospect it begins in a hazy thread stretching from Assyria into Egypt, from Egypt into Greece, from Greece to Rome—widening throughout Italy and Spain, then centering in Venice, and tracing clear and deep to Amsterdam—widening again into Germany and across to England, thence carried in "Mayflowers" to America.

That remark of Charles Dudley Warner, once near neighbor to Mark Twain, that there is no culture west of Buffalo, was indelicate if not unkind; and residents of Omaha aver that it is open to argument. But the fact stands beyond cavil that what art we possess is traceable to our masters, the Dutch.

It must be admitted that the art of printing was first practised at Mayence on the Rhine, leaving the Chinese out of the equation; but it had to travel around down through Italy before it reached perfection. And its universality and usefulness were not fully developed until it had swung around to Holland and was given by the Dutch back to Germany and the world. And as with printing, so with music. Germany has specialized on music. She has succeeded, but it is because Holland gave her lessons.

During the fore part of the Seventeenth Century, there lived in Antwerp, Ludvig van Biethofen, grandfather of the genius known as Beethoven. A life-size portrait of him can be seen in the Plantin Musee, and if you did not know that the picture was painted before Beethoven was born, you would say at once, "Beethoven!" There is a look of stern endurance, as if the artist had admired Rembrandt's "Burgomaster" a little too well, yet that sturdiness belonged to the Master, too; and there are the abstracted far-away look, the touch of proud melancholy, and the becoming unkemptness that we know so well.

The child is grandfather to the man. Beethoven bore slight resemblance to his immediate parents, but in his talent, habits and all of his mental traits, he closely resembled this sturdy

11

Dutchman who composed, sang, led the military band, and played the organ at the Church of Saint Jacques in Antwerp.

Being ambitious, Ludvig van Biethofen, while yet a young man, moved to Bonn, the home of Clement Augustus, Archbishop-Elector of Cologne.

The chief business of elector was, in case of necessity, to elect a King. America borrowed the elector idea from Germany. But our "electoral college" is a degenerate political appendicle that is continued, because, in borrowing plans of government, we took good and bad alike, not knowing there was a difference. The elector scheme in the United States is occasionally valuable for defeating the will of the people in case of a popular majority.

In justice, however, let me say that the original argument of the Colonists was that the people should not vote directly for President, because the candidate might live a long way off, and the voter could not know whether he was fit or not. So they let the citizen vote for a wise and honest elector he knew.

The result is that we all now know the candidates for President, but we do not know the electors. The electoral college in America is just about as useful as the two buttons on the back of a man's coat, put there originally to support a sword-belt. We have discarded the sword, yet we cling to our buttons.

But the electors of Germany, in days agone, had a well-defined use. The people were not, at first, troubled to elect them—the King did that himself, and then as one good turn deserves another, the electors agreed to elect the successor the King designated, when death should compel him to abdicate. Then to fill in the time between elections, the electors did the business of the King. It will thus be seen that every elector was really a sort of King himself, governing his little State, amenable to no one but the King.

And so the chief business of the elector was to keep the people in his diocese loyal to the King.

There have always existed three ways of keeping the people loving and loyal. One is to leave them alone, to trust them and not to interfere. This plan, however, has very seldom been practised, because the politicians regard the public as a cow to be milked, and something must be done to make it stand quiet.

So they try Plan Number Two, which consists in hypnotizing the public by means of shows, festivals, parades, prizes and many paid speeches, sermons and editorials, wherein and whereby the public is told how much is being done for it, and how fortunate it is in being protected and wisely cared for by its divinely appointed guardians. Then the band strikes up, the flags are waved, three passes are made, one to the right and two to the left; and we, being completely under the hypnosis, hurrah ourselves hoarse.

Plan Number Three is a very ancient one and is always held back to be used in case Number Two fails. It is for the benefit of the people who do not pass readily under hypnotic control. If there are too many of these, they have been known to pluck up courage and answer back to the speeches, sermons and editorials. Sometimes they refuse to hurrah when the bass-drum plays, in which case they have occasionally been arrested for contumacy and contravention by stocky men, in wide-awake hats, who lead the strenuous life. This Plan Number Three provides for an armed force that shall overawe, if necessary, all who are not hypnotized. The army is used for two purposes—to coerce disturbers at home, and to get up a war at a distance, and thus distract attention from the troubles near at hand. Napoleon used to say that the only sure cure for internal dissension was a foreign war: this would draw the disturbers away, on the plea of patriotism, so they would win enough outside loot to satisfy them, or else they would all get killed, it really didn't matter much; and as for loot, if it was taken from foreigners, there was no sin.

A careful analyst might here say that Plan Number Three is only a variation of Plan Number Two—the end being gained by hypnotic effects in either event, for the army is conscripted from the people to use against the people, just as you turn steam from a boiler into the fire-box to increase the draft. Possibly this is true, but I have introduced this digression, anyway, only to show that the original office of elector was a wise and beneficent function of the Government, and could be revived with profit in America, to replace the outworn and useless vermiformis that we now possess in way of an electoral college.

When Kings allowed Church and State to separate they made a grave mistake. With the two united, as they were until a more recent time, they held a cinch on both the souls and the bodies of their subjects.

In the good old days in Germany the elector was always an archbishop. Our bishops now are a weakling lot. With no army to back their edicts the people smile at their proclamations, try on their shovel hats, and laugh at their gaiters. Or if they be Methodist bishops, who are only make-believe bishops, having slipped the cable that bound them to the past, we pound them familiarly on the back and address them as "Bish."

Clement Augustus, Elector of Cologne, maintained a court that vied with royalty itself. In his household were two hundred servants. He had coachmen, footmen, cooks, messengers, a bodyguard, musicians, poets and artists who hastened to do his bidding. He patronized all the arts, made a pet of science, offered a reward for the transmutation of metals, dabbled in astrology and practised palmistry.

Into this brilliant court came the strong and masterful Ludvig van Biethofen.

In a year his gracious presence, superb voice and rare skill as a musician, pushed him to the front and into favor with the powers, with a yearly salary of four hundred guilders. The history of this man is a deal better raw stock for a romance than the life of his grandson.

From Seventeen Hundred Thirty-two, when he entered the court as an unknown and ordinary musician with an acceptable tenor voice, to Seventeen Hundred Sixty-one, when he was Kapellmeister and a member of the private council of the Elector, his life was a steady march successward. Strong men were needed then as now, and his promotion was deserved. Various accounts and mention of this man are to be found, and one contemporary described him as he appeared at sixty. The only mark of age he carried was his flowing white hair. His smoothly shaven face showed the strong features of a man of thirty-five; and his carriage, actions and superb grace as an orchestra-leader made him a conspicuous figure in any company.

Ludvig van Biethofen had one son, Johann by name. This boy resembled his gifted father very little, and his training was such that he early fell a victim to arrested development.

If a parent does everything for a child, the child probably will never do anything for himself. It is Nature's plan—she seems to think that no one needs strength excepting the struggler, and being kind she comes to his rescue; but the man who puts forth no effort remains a weakling to the end.

Johann placed success beyond his reach very early in life by putting an enemy into his mouth to steal away his brains. His marriage to a daughter of a cook in Ehrenbreitstein Castle did not stop his waywardness, or give him decision as was hoped. Marriage as a scheme of reformation is not always a success, and women who lend themselves to it take great chances.

Mary Magdalena was a widow, and some say possessed of wiles. That she was beneath Johann in social station, but beyond him in actual worth, there is no doubt. And whether she snared the incautious man, or whether the marriage was arranged by the elder Biethofen as a diplomatic move in the interests of morality, matters little. The end justifies the means; and as a net result of this mating, without putting forward the circumstance as a precedent to be religiously followed, the world has Beethoven and his work.

A plate affixed to Number Five Hundred Fifteen Bonngasse, Bonn, gives the birth of Ludwig van Beethoven as December Seventeenth, Seventeen Hundred Seventy. He was the second-born child of his mother, and after him came a goodly assortment of boys and girls. Two of his brothers lived to exercise a sinister influence over the life of the Master, and to darken days that should have been luminous with love. Little Ludwig was the pet and pride of the grandfather. The grandfather had even insisted that the baby should bear his name. Disappointment in his own child caused him to center his love in the grandchild. This instinct that makes men long to live again in the lives of their children—is it reaching out for immortality? And as the grandfather virtually supported the household, he was allowed to have his own way, and indeed that strong, yet cheery will was not to be opposed. The old man prophesied what the boy would do, just as love ever does, and has done, since the world began.

But only in his dreams was Ludvig van Biethofen to know of the success of his namesake. When the boy was scarce four years old, the old man passed away. The place in the orchestra that Johann held through favor was soon forfeited, and times of pinching poverty followed, and sorrows came like the gathering of a winter night.

Have you never shared the mocking shame and biting pain of a drunkard's household? Then God grant you never may. When the world withdraws its faith from a man through his own imbecility, and employment is denied; when promises are unkept; when order and system are gone, and foresight fled, and loud accusation, threat and contumely vary their strident tones with maudlin protestations of affection, and vows made to be broken, easily change to curses; when the fire dies on the hearth, and children huddle in bed in the daytime for warmth; when the scanty food that is found is eaten ravenously, and blanching fear comes when a heavy tread and fumbling at the lock are heard in the hall—these things challenge language for fit expression and cause words to falter.

The moody and dispirited Johann one day conceived a bright thought—a thought so vivid that for the moment it cleared the cobwebs from his mind and sobered his boozy brain—the genius of his five-year-old boy should be exploited to retrieve his battered fortunes!

The child was already showing signs of musical talent; and diligent practise was now begun. Several chums at the beer-gardens were interviewed and great plans unfolded in beery enthusiasm. The services of several of these men were secured as tutors, and one of them, Pfeiffer, took lodgings with the Biethofens, and paid for bed and board in music-lessons.

A new thought is purifying, ideas are hygienic; and already things had begun to look brighter for the household. It wasn't exactly prosperity, but Johann had found a place in the band, and was earning as much as three dollars a week, which amount for two weeks running he brought home and placed in his wife's lap.

But things were grievous for young Beethoven: he had two taskmasters, his father and Pfeiffer. One gave him lessons on the violin in the morning, and the other took him to a tavern where there was a clavichord and made him play all the afternoon.

Then occasionally Johann and Pfeiffer would come home at two o'clock in the morning from a concert where they had been playing and where the wine was red and also free, and they would drag the poor child from his bed to make him play. This was followed up until the boy's mother rebelled, and on one occasion Pfeiffer and Johann were sent to the military hospital and dry-docked for repairs.

On the whole, this man Pfeiffer was kindly and usually capable. In after-years Beethoven testified to the valuable assistance he had received from him; and when Pfeiffer had grown old and helpless, Beethoven sent funds to him by the publishers, Simrock.

Young Ludwig was a stocky, sturdy youth, decidedly Dutch in his characteristics, with no nerves to speak of, else he would have laid him down and died of heart-chill and neglect, as did four of his little brothers and sisters. But he stood the ordeals, and at parlor, tavern and beer-garden entertainments where he played, although his cheeks were often stained with tears, he took a sort of secret pride in being able to do things which even his father could not. And then he was always introduced as "Ludvig Biethofen, the grandchild of Ludvig van Biethofen," and this was no mean introduction. His appearance, even then, bore strong resemblance to the lost and lamented grandfather; and Van den Eeden, the Court Organist, in loving remembrance of his Antwerp friend, took the lad into his keeping and gave him lessons. When Van den Eeden retired, Neefe, his successor, took a kindly interest in the boy and even protected him from his father and the zealous Pfeiffer. So well was the boy thought of that when he was twelve years of age Neefe established him as his deputy at the chapel organ.

Shortly after this, the new Elector, Max Friedrich, bestowed on "Louis van Beethoven, my well-beloved player upon the organ and clavichord, a stipend of one hundred fifty florins a year, and if his talent doth increase with his years the amount is to be also increased."

In token of the Elector's recognition Beethoven wrote three sonatas, the earliest of his compositions, and dedicated them to Max Friedrich in Seventeen Hundred Eighty-two.

In Seventeen Hundred Eighty-four, Elector Max Friedrich died, and Max Franz was appointed to take his place. His inauguration was the signal for a renewal of musical and artistic activity. Concerts, shows and military pageants followed the installation. In a list of court appointments we find that Louis van Beethoven is put down as "second organist" with a salary of forty-five pounds a year. Below this is Johann Beethoven with a salary of thirty pounds a year. And in one of the court journals mention is made of Johann Beethoven with the added line, "father of Ludwig Beethoven," showing even then the man's source of distinction.

In Seventeen Hundred Eighty-seven, when in his eighteenth year, Beethoven made a visit to Vienna in company with several musicians from the Elector's court at Bonn. This visit was a memorable event in the life of the Master, every detail of which was deeply etched upon his memory, to be effaced only by death.

It was on this visit to Vienna that he met Mozart, and played for him. Mozart gave due attention, and when the player had ceased he turned to the company and said, "Keep your eye on this youth—he will yet make a noise in the world!" The remark, if closely analyzed, reveals itself as noncommittal; and although it has been bruited as praise the round world over, it was probably an electrotyped expression, used daily; for great musicians are called upon at every turn to listen to prodigies. I once attended "rhetoricals" where the Honorable Chauncey M. Depew was present. Being called upon to "make a few remarks," the Senator from New York arose and referred to one of the speeches given by a certain sophomore as "unlike anything I ever heard before!" Genius very seldom recognizes genius.

Beethoven had a self-sufficiency, even at that early time, that stood him in good stead. He felt his power, and knew his worth. That steadfast, obstinate quality in his make-up was not in vain. He let others quote Mozart's remark; but he had matched himself against the Master, and was not abashed.

Kinship is a question of spirit and not a matter of blood. How often do we find persons who, in feeling, are absolutely strangers to their own brothers and sisters! Occasionally even parents fail to understand their children. The child may hunger for sympathy and love that the mother knows nothing of, and cry itself to sleep for a tenderness withheld. Later this same child may evolve aspirations and ambitions that seem to the other members of the family mere whims and vagaries to be laughed down, or stoutly endured, as the mood prompts.

Knowing these things, do we wonder at the question of long ago, "Who is my mother, and who are my brethren"? Beethoven was a beautiful brown thrush in a nest of cuckoos. He could sing and sing divinely, and the members of his household were glad because it brought an income in which they all shared.

About the year Seventeen Hundred Ninety-five, Beethoven went to Vienna, and as he had been heralded by several persons of influence, his reception was gracious. Charity has its periods of evolving into a fad, and at this time the fashion was musical entertainments in aid of this or that. Slight suspicions exist that these numerous entertainments were devised by fledgling musicians for their own aggrandizement, and possibly patrons fanned the philanthropic flame to help on their proteges. Beethoven was of too simple and guileless a nature to aid his fortunes with the help of any social jimmy, but we see he was soon in the full tide of local popularity. His ability as a composer, his virile presence, and his skill as a player, made his company desired. From playing first for charity, then at the houses of nobility, and next as a professional musician, he gradually mounted to the place to which his genius entitled him.

Then we find his brothers, Carl and Johann, appearing on the scene, with a fussy yet earnest intent to take care of the business affairs of their eccentric and absent-minded brother. Ludwig let himself fall into their way of thinking—it was easier than to oppose them—and they began to drive bargains with publishers and managers. Their intent was to sell for cash and in the highest market; and their strenuous effort after the Main Chance put their gifted brother in a bad plight before the world of art. Beethoven's brothers seized his very early and immature compositions and sold them without his consent or knowledge. So humiliated was Beethoven by seeing these productions of his childhood hawked about that he even instituted lawsuits to get them back that he might destroy them. To boom a genius and cash his spiritual assets is a grave and delicate task—perhaps it is one of those things that should be left undone. Much anguish did these rapacious brothers cause the divinely gifted brown thrush, and when they began to quarrel over the receipts between themselves, he begged them to go away and leave him in peace. He finally had to adopt the ruse of going back to Bonn with them, where he got them established in the apothecary business, before he dared manage his own affairs. But they were bad angels, and the wind of their wings withered the great man as they hovered around him down to the day of his death.

Then silence settled down upon Beethoven, and every piano was for him mute, and he, the maker of sweet sounds, could not hear his own voice, or catch the words that fell from the lips of those he loved, Fate seemed to have done her worst.

And so he wrote: "Forgive me then if you see me turn away when I would gladly mix with you. For me there is no recreation in human intercourse, no conversation, no sweet interchange of thought. In solitary exile I am compelled to live. When I approach strangers a feverish fear takes possession of me, for I know that I will be misunderstood. * * * But O God, Thou lookest down upon my inward soul! Thou knowest, and Thou seest that love for my fellowmen, and all kindly feeling have their abode here. Patience! I may get better—I may not—but I will endure all until Death shall claim me, and then joyously will I go!"

The man who could so express himself at twenty-eight years of age must have been a right brave and manly man. But art was his solace, as it should be to every soul that aspires to become.

Great genius and great love can never be separated—in fact I am not sure but that they are one and the same thing. But the object of his love separated herself from Beethoven when calamity lowered. What woman, young, bright, vigorous and fresh, with her face to the sunrising, would care to link her fair fate with that of a man sore-stricken by the hand of God!

And then there is always a doubt about the genius—isn't he only a fool after all!

Art was Beethoven's solace. Art is harmony, beauty and excellence. The province of art is to impart a sublime emotion. Beethoven's heart was filled with divine love—and all love is divine—and through his art he sought to express his love to others.

But his physical calamity made him the butt and byword of the heedless wherever he went. Within the sealed-up casements of his soul Beethoven heard the Heavenly Choir; and as he walked, bareheaded, upon the street, oblivious to all, centered in his own silent world, he would sometimes suddenly burst into song. At other times he would beat time, talk to himself and laugh aloud. His strange actions would often attract a crowd, and rude persons, ignorant of the man they mocked, would imitate him or make mirth for the bystanders, as they sought to engage him in conversation. At such times the Master might be dragged back to earth, and seeing the coarse faces and knowing the hopelessness of trying to make himself understood, he would retreat in terror.

Six months or more of each year were spent in the country in some obscure village about Vienna. There he could walk the woods and traverse the fields alone and unnoticed, and there, out under the open sky, much of his best work was done. The famous "Moonlight Sonata" was shaped on one of these lonely walks by night across the fields when the Master could shake his shaggy head, lift up his face to the sky, and cry aloud, all undisturbed. In the recesses of his imagination he saw the sounds. There are men to whom sounds are invisible symbols of forms and colors.

The law of compensation never rests. Everything conspired to drive Beethoven in upon his art—it was his refuge and retreat. When love spurned him, and misunderstandings with kinsmen came, and lawsuits and poverty added their weight of woe, he fell back upon music, and out under the stars he listened to the sonatas of God. Next day he wrote them out as best he could, always regretting that his translations were not quite perfect. He was ever stung with a noble discontent, and in times of exaltation there ran in his deaf ears the words, "Arise and get thee hence, for this is not thy rest!"

And so his work was in a constant ascending scale. Richard Wagner has acknowledged his indebtedness to Beethoven in several essays, and in many ways. In fact it is not too much to say that Beethoven was the spiritual parent of Wagner. From his admiration of Beethoven, Wagner developed the strong, sturdy, independent quality of his nature that led to his exile—and his success.

Behold the face of Ludwig Beethoven—is there not something Titanic about it? What selfness, what will, what resolve, what power! And those tear-stained eyes—have they not seen sights of which no tongue can tell, nor tongue make plain? His life of solitude helped foster the independence of his nature, and kept his mind clear and free from all the idle gossip of the rabble. He went his way alone, and played court fool to no titled and alleged nobility. The democracy of the man is not our least excuse for honoring him. He was one with the plain people of earth, and the only aristocracy he acknowledged was the aristocracy of intellect.

In the work done after his fortieth year there is greater freedom, an ease and an increased strength, with a daring quality which uplifts and gives you courage. The tragic interest and intense emotionalism are gone, and you behold a resignation and the success that wins by yielding. The man is no longer at war with destiny. There is no struggle.

We pay for everything we receive—nay, all things can be obtained if we but pay the price. One of the very few Emancipated Men in America bought redemption from the bondage of selfish ambition at a terrible price. Years and years ago he was in the Rocky Mountains, rough, uneducated, heedless of all that makes for righteousness. This man was caught in a snowstorm, on the mountainside. He lost his way, became dazed with cold and fell exhausted in the snow. When found by his companions the next day, death had nearly claimed him. But skilful help brought him back to life, yet the frost had killed the circulation in his feet. Both legs were amputated just below the knees.

This changed the current of the man's life. Footraces, boxing-matches and hunting of big game were out of the question. The man turned to books and art and questions of science and sociology.

Thirty summers have come and gone. This gentle, sympathetic and loving man now walks with a cane, and few know of his disability and of his artificial feet. Speaking of his spiritual rebirth, this man of splendid intellect said to me, with a smile, "It cost me my feet, but it was worth the price."

I shed no maudlin tears over the misfortunes of Beethoven. He was what he was because of what he endured. He grew strong by bearing burdens. All things are equalized. By the Cross is the world redeemed. God be praised, it is all good!

A CHAPTER FROM
Little Journeys to the Homes of Great Musicians, 1894

LUDWIG VAN BEETHOVEN

By Harriette Brower

The Shakespeare of the realm of music, as he has been called, first saw the light on December 16, 1770, in the little University town of Bonn, on the Rhine. His father, Johann Beethoven, belonged to the court band of the Elector of Cologne. The family were extremely poor. The little room, where the future great master was born, was so low, that a good-sized man could barely stand upright in it. Very small it was too, and not very light either, as it was at the back of the building and looked out on a walled garden.

The fame of young Mozart, who was acclaimed everywhere as a marvellous prodigy, had naturally reached the father's ears. He decided to train the little Ludwig as a pianist, so that he should also be hailed as a prodigy and win fame and best of all money for the poverty-stricken family. So the tiny child was made to practice scales and finger exercises for hours together. He was a musically gifted child, but how he hated those everlasting tasks of finger technic, when he longed to join his little companions, who could run and play in the sunshine. If he stopped his practice to rest and dream a bit, the stern face of his father would appear at the doorway, and a harsh voice would call out, "Ludwig! what are you doing? Go on with your exercises at once. There will be no soup for you till they are finished."

The father, though harsh and stern, wished his boy to have as thorough a knowledge of music as his means would permit. The boy was also sent to the public school, where he picked up reading and writing, but did not make friends very quickly with the other children. The fact was the child seemed wholly absorbed in music; of music he dreamed constantly; in the companionship of music he never could be lonely.

When Ludwig was nine his father, regarding him with satisfaction and some pride, declared he could teach him no more—and another master must be found. Those childhood years of hard toil had resulted in remarkable progress, even with the sort of teaching he had received. The circumstances of the family had not improved, for poverty had become acute, as the father became more and more addicted to drink. Just at this time, a new lodger appeared, who was something of a musician, and arranged to teach the boy in part payment for his room. Ludwig wondered if he would turn out to be a more severe taskmaster than his father had been. The times and seasons when his instruction was given were at least unusual. Tobias Pfeiffer, as the new lodger was called, soon discovered that father Beethoven generally spent his evenings at the tavern. As an act of kindness, to keep his drunken landlord out of the way of the police, Tobias used to go to the tavern late at night and bring him safely home. Then he would go to the bedside of the sleeping boy, and awake him by telling him it was time for practice. The two would go to the living room, where they would play together for several hours, improvising on original themes and playing duets. This went on for about a year; meanwhile Ludwig studied Latin, French, Italian and logic. He also had organ lessons.

Things were going from bad to worse in the Beethoven home, and in the hope of bettering these unhappy conditions, Frau Beethoven undertook a trip through Holland with her boy, hoping that his playing in the homes of the wealthy might produce some money. The tour was successful in that it relieved the pressing necessities of the moment, but the sturdy, independent spirit of the boy showed itself even then. "The Dutch are very stingy, and I shall take care not to trouble them again," he remarked to a friend.

The boy Ludwig could play the organ fairly well, as he had studied it with Christian Neefe, who was organist at the Court church. He also could play the piano with force and finish, read well at sight and knew nearly the whole of Bach's "Well Tempered Clavichord." This was a pretty good record for a boy of 11, who, if he went on as he had begun, it was said, would become a second Mozart.

Neefe was ordered to proceed with the Elector and Court to Münster, which meant to leave his organ in Bonn for a time. Before starting he called Ludwig to him and told him of his intended absence. "I must have an assistant to take my place at the organ here. Whom do you think I should appoint?" Seeing the boy had no inkling of his meaning, he continued: "I have thought of an assistant, one I am sure I can trust,—and that is you, Ludwig."

The honor was great, for a boy of eleven and a half. To conduct the service, and receive the respect and deference due the position, quite overwhelmed the lad. Honors of this kind were very pleasant, but, alas, there was no money attached to the position, and this was what the straitened family needed most sorely. The responsibilities of the position and the confidence of Neefe spurred Ludwig on to a passion of work which nothing could check. He began to compose; three sonatas for the pianoforte were written about this time. Before completing his thirteenth year, Ludwig obtained his first official appointment from the Elector; he became what is called cembalist in the orchestra, which meant that he had to play the piano in the orchestra, and conduct the band at rehearsals. With this appointment there was no salary attached either, and it was not until a year later when he was made second organist to the Court, under the new Elector, Max Franz, that he began to receive a small salary, equal to about sixty-five dollars a year. We have seen that the straits of the family had not prevented Ludwig from pursuing his musical studies with great ardor. With his present attainments and his ambition for higher achievements, he longed to leave the little town of Bonn, and see something of the great world. Vienna was the center of the musical life of Germany; the boy dreamed of this magical city by day as he went about his routine of work, and by night as he lay on his poor narrow cot. Like Haydn, Vienna was the goal of his ambition. When a kind friend, knowing his great longing, came forward with an offer to pay the expenses of the journey, the lad knew his dream was to become a reality. In Vienna he would see the first composers of the day; best of all he would see and meet the divine Mozart, the greatest of them all.

Ludwig, now seventeen, set out for the city of his dreams with the brightest anticipations. On his arrival in Vienna he went at once to Mozart's house. He was received most kindly and asked to play, but Mozart seemed preoccupied and paid but little attention. Ludwig, seeing this stopped playing and asked for a theme on which to improvise. Mozart gave a simple theme, and Beethoven, taking the slender thread, worked it up with so much feeling and power, that Mozart, who was now all attention and astonishment, stepped into the next room, where some friends were waiting for him, and said, "Pay attention to this young man; he will make a noise in the world some day."

Shortly after his return home he was saddened by the loss of his good, kind, patient mother, and a few months later his little sister Margaretha passed away. No doubt these sorrows were expressed in some of his most beautiful compositions. But brighter days followed the dark ones. He became acquainted with the Breuning family, a widow lady and four children, three boys and a girl, all young people. The youngest boy and the girl became his pupils, and all were very fond of him. He would stay at their house for days at a time and was always treated as one of the family. They were cultured people, and in their society Beethoven's whole nature expanded. He began to take an interest in the literature of his own country and in English authors as well. All his spare time was given to reading and composition. A valuable acquaintance with the young Count

Von Waldstein was made about this time. The Count called one day and found the composer at his old worn out piano, surrounded by signs of abject poverty. It went to his heart to see that the young man, whose music he so greatly admired should have to struggle for the bare necessities of life while he himself enjoyed every luxury. It seemed to him terribly unjust. He feared to offend the composer's self-respect by sending him money, but shortly after the call Beethoven was made happy by the gift of a fine new piano, in place of his old one. He was very grateful for this friendship and later dedicated to the Count one of his finest sonatas, the Op. 53, known as the "Waldstein Sonata."

With a view of aiding the growth of the opera, and operatic art, the Elector founded a national theater, and Beethoven was appointed viola player in the orchestra besides still being assistant organist in the chapel. In July, 1792, the band arranged a reception for Haydn, who was to pass through Bonn on his way from London, where he had had a wonderful success, to his home in Vienna. Beethoven seized the opportunity to show the master a cantata he had just composed. Haydn praised the work and greatly encouraged the young musician to go forward in his studies. The Elector, hearing of Haydn's words of praise, felt that Beethoven should have the chance to develop his talents that he might be able to produce greater works. Therefore he decided to send the young composer, at his own expense, to study strict counterpoint with Haydn. He was now twenty-two and his compositions already published had brought him considerable fame and appreciation in his vicinity. Now he was to have wider scope for his gifts.

He bade farewell to Bonn in November of this year and set out a second time for the city of his dreams—Vienna. He was never to see Bonn again. He arrived in Vienna comparatively unknown, but his fine piano playing and wonderful gift for improvising greatly impressed all who heard him. He constantly played in the homes of the wealthy aristocracy. Many who heard him play, engaged lessons and he was well on the road to social success. Yet his brusque manners often antagonized his patrons. He made no effort to please or conciliate; he was obstinate and self-willed. In spite of all this, the innate nobleness and truth of his character retained the regard of men and women belonging to the highest ranks of society. With the Prince and Princess Lichnowsky Beethoven shortly became very intimate, and was invited to stay at the Palace. The Princess looked after his personal comfort with as motherly an affection as Madame Breuning had done. The etiquette of the Palace however, offended Ludwig's love of Bohemianism, especially the dressing for dinner at a certain time. He took to dining at a tavern quite frequently, and finally engaged lodgings. The Prince and his good lady, far from taking offense at this unmannerly behavior, forgave it and always kept for Beethoven a warm place in their hearts, while he, on his part was sincere in his affection for his kind friends.

Beethoven began his lessons with Haydn, but they did not seem to get on well together. The pupil thought the master did not give him enough time and attention. When Haydn went to England, about a year after the lessons began, Beethoven studied with several of the best musicians of the city, both in playing and composition. Albrechtsberger, one of these, was a famous contrapuntist of his time, and the student gained much from his teaching. The young musician was irresistible when he seated himself at the piano to extemporize. "His improvisating was most brilliant and striking," wrote Carl Czerny, a pupil of Beethoven. "In whatever company he might be, he knew how to produce such an effect upon the listeners that frequently all eyes would be wet, and some listeners would sob; there was something wonderful in his expressive style, the beauty and originality of his ideas and his spirited way of playing." Strange to say the emotion he roused in his hearers seemed to find no response in Beethoven himself. He would sometimes laugh at it, at other times he would resent it, saying, "We artists don't want tears, we want applause." These expressions however only concealed his inner feelings—for he was very sympathetic with those friends he loved. His anger, though sharp, was of short duration, but his suspicions of those whose confidence he had won by his genius and force of character, were the cause of much suffering to himself and others.

Beethoven in appearance was short and stockily built; his face was not at all good looking. It is said he was generally meanly dressed and was homely, but full of nobility, fine feeling and highly cultivated. The eyes were black and bright, and they dilated, when the composer was lost in thought, in a way that made him look inspired. A mass of dark hair surmounted a high broad forehead. He often looked gloomy, but when he smiled it was with a radiant brightness. His hands were strong and the fingers short and pressed out with much practise. He was very particular about hand position when playing. As a conductor he made many movements, and is said to have crouched below the desk in soft passages; in Crescendos he would gradually lift himself up until at the loudest parts he would rise to his full height with arms extended, even springing into the air, as though he would float in space.

Beethoven as a teacher, showed none of the impatience and carelessness that were seen in his personal habits. He insisted on a pupil repeating the passage carefully a number of times, until it could be played to his satisfaction. He did not seem to mind a few wrong notes, but the pupil must not fail to grasp the meaning or put in the right expression, or his anger would be aroused. The first was an accident, the other would be a lack of knowledge of feeling.

Beethoven loved nature as much or more than any musician ever did. How he hailed the spring because he knew the time would soon come when he could close the door of his lodgings in the hot city, and slip away to some quiet spot and hold sweet communion with nature. A forest was a paradise, where he could ramble among the trees and dream. Or he would select a tree where a forking branch would form a seat near the ground.

He would climb up and sit in it for hours, lost in thought. Leaning against the trunk of a lime tree, his eyes fixed upon the network of leaves and branches above him, he sketched the plan of his oratorio "The Mount of Olives"; also that of his one opera "Fidelio," and the third Symphony, known as the "Eroica." He wrote to a friend, "No man loves the country more than I. Woods, trees and rocks give the response which man requires. Every tree seems to say 'Holy, holy.'"

Already, as a young man, symptoms of deafness began to appear, and the fear of becoming a victim of this malady made the composer more sensitive than ever. He was not yet thirty when this happened, and believing his life work at an end, he became deeply depressed. Various treatments were tried for increasing deafness; at one time it seemed to be cured by the skill of Dr. Schmidt, to whom out of gratitude he dedicated his Septet, arranged as a Trio. By his advice the composer went for the summer of 1820 to the little village of Heiligenstadt (which means Holy City) in the hope that the calm, sweet environment would act as a balm to his troubled mind. During this period of rest and quiet his health improved somewhat, but from now on he had to give up conducting his works, on account of his deafness.

It may be thought that one so reticent and retiring, of such hasty temper and brusque manners, would scarcely be attracted to women. But Beethoven, it is said, was very susceptible to the charm of the opposite sex. He was however, most careful and high-souled in all his relations with women. He was frequently in love, but it was usually a Platonic affection. For the Countess Julie Guicciardi he protested the most passionate love, which was in a measure returned. She was doubtless his "immortal beloved," whose name vibrates through the Adagio of the "Moonlight Sonata," which is dedicated to her. He wrote her the most adoring letters; but the union, which he seemed to desire so intensely, was never brought about, though the reason is not known. For Bettina von Arnim, Goethe's little friend, he conceived a tender affection. Another love of his was for the Countess Marie Erdödy, to whom he dedicated the two fine Trios, Op. 70, but this was also a purely Platonic affection. The composer was unfortunate in his attachments, for the objects were always of a much higher social standing than himself. As he constantly associated with people of rank and culture, it was natural that the young girl nobly born, with all the fascinations of the high bred aristocrat, should attract him far more than the ordinary woman of his own class. And thus it happened that several times he staked his chances of happiness on a love he knew could never be consummated. Yet no one needed a kind, helpful, sympathetic wife more than did our poet-musician. She would have soothed his sensitive soul when he suffered from fancied wrongs, shielded him from intrusion, shared his sorrows and triumphs, and attended to his house-keeping arrangements, which were always in a sad state of confusion. This blissful state was seemingly not for him. It was best for the great genius to devote himself wholly to his divine art, and to create those masterpieces which will always endure.

In 1804 Beethoven completed one of his greatest symphonies, the "Eroica." He made a sketch, as we have seen, two years before. He had intended it to honor Napoleon, to whose character and career he was greatly attracted. But when Napoleon entered Paris in triumph and was proclaimed Emperor, Beethoven's worship was turned to contempt. He seized the symphony, tore the little page to shreds and flung the work to the other end of the room. It was a long time before he would look at the music again, but finally, he consented to publish it under the title by which it is now known.

When we consider the number and greatness of Beethoven's compositions we stand aghast at the amount of labor he accomplished. "I live only in my music," he wrote, "and no sooner is one thing done than the next is begun. I often work at two or three things at once." Music was his language of expression, and through his music we can reach his heart and know the man as he really was. At heart he was a man capable of loving deeply and most worthy to be loved.

Of the composer's two brothers, one had passed away and had left his boy Carl, named after himself, as a solemn charge, to be brought up by Uncle Ludwig as his own son. The composer took up this task generously and unselfishly. He was happy to have the little lad near him, one of his own kin to love. But as Carl grew to young manhood he proved to be utterly unworthy of all this affection. He treated his good uncle shamefully, stole money from him, though he had been always generously supplied with it, and became a disgrace to the family. There is no doubt that his nephew's dissolute habits saddened the master's life, estranged him from his friends and hastened his death.

How simple and modest was this great master, in face of his mighty achievements! He wrote to a friend in 1824: "I feel as if I had scarcely written more than a few notes." These later years had been more than full of work and anxiety. Totally deaf, entirely thrown in upon himself, often weak and ill, the master kept on creating work after work of the highest beauty and grandeur.

Ludwig van Beethoven passed from this plane March 26, 1827, having recently completed his fifty-sixth year, and was laid to rest in the Währing Cemetery near Vienna. Unlike Mozart, he was buried with much honor. Twenty thousand people followed him to his grave. Among them was Schubert, who had visited him on his deathbed, and was one of the torch bearers. Several of the Master's compositions were sung by a choir of male voices, accompanied by trombones. At the grave Hummel laid three laurel wreaths on the casket.

A Chapter from
*The World's Great Men of Music -
Story-Lives of Master Musicians,*1922

BEETHOVEN

By George T. Ferris

I

The name and memory of this composer awaken, in the heart of the lover of music, sentiments of the deepest reverence and admiration. His life was so marked with affliction and so isolated as to make him, in his environment of conditions as a composer, a unique figure.

The principal fact which made the exterior life of Beethoven so bare of the ordinary pleasures that brighten and sweeten existence, his total deafness, greatly enriched his spiritual life. Music finally became to him a purely intellectual conception, for he was without any sensual enjoyment of its effects. To this Samson of music, for whom the ear was like the eye to other men, Milton's lines may indeed well apply:

> "Oh! dark, dark, dark, amid the blaze of noon!
> Irrecoverably dark—total eclipse,
> Without all hope of day!
> Oh first created Beam, and thou, great Word,
> 'Let there be light,' and light was over all,
> Why am I thus bereaved thy prime decree
> The sun to me is dark."

To his severe affliction we owe alike many of the defects of his character and the splendors of his genius. All his powers, concentrated into a spiritual focus, wrought such things as lift him into a solitary greatness. The world has agreed to measure this man as it measures Homer, Dante, and Shakespeare. We do not compare him with others.

Beethoven had the reputation among his contemporaries of being harsh, bitter, suspicious, and unamiable. There is much to justify this in the circumstances of his life; yet our readers will discover much to show, on the other hand, how deep, strong, and tender was the heart which was so wrung and tortured, and wounded to the quick by—

"The slings and arrows of outrageous fortune."

Weber gives a picture of Beethoven: "The square Cyclopean figure attired in a shabby coat with torn sleeves." Everybody will remember his noble, austere face, as seen in the numerous prints: the square, massive head, with the forest of rough hair; the strong features, so furrowed with the marks of passion and sadness; the eyes, with their look of introspection and insight; the whole expression of the countenance as of an ancient prophet. Such was the impression made by Beethoven on all who saw him, except in his moods of fierce wrath, which toward the last were not uncommon, though short-lived. A sorely tried, sublimely gifted man, he met his fate stubbornly, and worked out his great mission with all his might and main, through long years of weariness and trouble. Posterity has rewarded him by enthroning him on the highest peaks of musical fame.

II

Ludwig van Beethoven was born at Bonn, in 1770. It is a singular fact that at an early age he showed the deepest distaste for music, unlike the other great composers, who evinced their bent from their earliest years. His father was obliged to whip him severely before he would consent to sit down at the harpsichord; and it was not till he was past ten that his genuine interest in music showed itself. His first compositions displayed his genius. Mozart heard him play them, and said, "Mind, you will hear that boy talked of." Haydn, too, met Beethoven for the first and only time when the former was on his way to England, and recognized his remarkable powers. He gave him a few lessons in composition, and was after that anxious to claim the young Titan as a pupil.

"Yes," growled Beethoven, who for some queer reason never liked Haydn, "I had some lessons of him, indeed, but I was not his disciple. I never learned anything from him."

Beethoven made a profound impression even as a youth on all who knew him. Aside from the palpable marks of his power, there was an indomitable *hauteur*, a mysterious, self-wrapped air as of one constantly communing with the invisible, an unconscious assertion of mastery about him, which strongly impressed the imagination.

At the very outset of his career, when life promised all fair and bright things to him, two comrades linked themselves to him, and ever after that refused to give him up—grim poverty and still grimmer disease. About the same time that he lost a fixed salary through the death of his friend the Elector of Cologne, he began to grow deaf. Early in 1800, walking one day in the woods with his devoted friend and pupil, Ferdinand Ries, he disclosed the sad secret to him that the whole joyous world of sound was being gradually closed up to him; the charm of the human voice, the notes of the woodland birds, the sweet babblings of Nature, jargon to others, but intelligible to genius, the full-born splendors of *heard* music—all, all were fast receding from his grasp.

Beethoven was extraordinarily sensitive to the influences of Nature. Before his disease became serious he writes: "I wander about here with music-paper among the hills, and dales, and valleys, and scribble a good deal. No man on earth can love the country as I do." But one of Nature's most delightful modes of speech to man was soon to be utterly lost to him. At last he became so deaf that the most stunning crash of thunder or the *fortissimo* of the full orchestra were to him as if they were not. His bitter, heartrending cry of agony, when he became convinced that the misfortune was irremediable, is full of eloquent despair: "As autumn leaves wither and fall, so are my hopes blighted. Almost as I came, I depart. Even the lofty courage, which so often animated me in the lovely days of summer, is gone forever. O Providence! vouchsafe me one day of pure felicity! How long have I been estranged from the glad echo of true joy! When, O my God! when shall I feel it again in the temple of Nature and man? Never!"

And the small-souled, mole-eyed gossips and critics called him hard, churlish, and cynical—him, for whom the richest thing in Nature's splendid dower had been obliterated, except a soul, which never in its deepest sufferings lost its noble faith in God and man, or allowed its indomitable courage to be one whit weakened. That there were periods of utterly rayless despair and gloom we may guess; but not for long did Beethoven's great nature cower before its evil genius.

III

Within three years, from 1805 to 1808, Beethoven composed some of his greatest works: the oratorio of "The Mount of Olives," the opera of "Fidelio," and the two noble symphonies, "Pastorale" and "Eroica," besides a large number of concertos, sonatas, songs, and other occasional pieces. However gloomy the externals of his life, his creative activities knew no cessation.

The "Sinfonia Eroica," the "Choral" only excepted, is the longest of the immortal nine, and is one of the greatest examples of musical portraiture extant. All the great composers from Handel to Wagner have attempted what is called descriptive music with more or less success, but never have musical genius and skill achieved a result so admirable in its relation to its purpose and by such strictly legitimate means as in this work.

"The 'Eroica,'" says a great writer, "is an attempt to draw a musical portrait of an historical character—a great statesman, a great general, a noble individual; to represent in music—Beethoven's own language—what M. Thiers has given in words and Paul Delaroche in painting." Of Beethoven's success another writer has said: "It wants no title to tell its meaning, for throughout the symphony the hero is visibly portrayed."

It is anything but difficult to realize why Beethoven should have admired the first Napoleon. Both the soldier and musician were made of that sturdy stuff which would and did defy the world; and it is not strange that Beethoven should have desired in some way—and he knew of no better course than through his art—to honor one so characteristically akin to himself, and who at that time was the most prominent man in Europe. Beethoven began the work in 1802, and in 1804 it was completed, and bore the following title:

Sinfonia grande
"Napoleon Bonaparte"
1804 in August
del Sigr
Louis van Beethoven
Sinfonia 3.
Op. 55.

This was copied and the original score dispatched to the embassador for presentation, while Beethoven retained the copy. Before the composition was laid before Napoleon, however, the great general had accepted the title of Emperor. No sooner did Beethoven hear of this from his pupil Ries than he started up in a rage, and exclaimed: "After all, then, he's nothing but an ordinary mortal! He will trample the rights of men under his feet!" saying which, he rushed to his table, seized the copy of the score, and tore the title-page completely off. From this time Beethoven hated Napoleon, and never again spoke of him in connection with the symphony until he heard of his death in St. Helena, when he observed, "I have already composed music for this calamity," evidently referring to the "Funeral March" in this symphony.

The opera of "Fidelio," which he composed about the same time, may be considered, in the severe sense of a great and symmetrical musical work, the finest lyric drama ever written, with the possible exception of Gluck's "Orpheus and Eurydice" and "Iphigenia in Tauris." It is rarely performed, because its broad, massive, and noble effects are beyond the capacity of most singers, and belong to the domain of pure music, demanding but little alliance with the artistic clap-trap of startling scenery and histrionic extravagance. Yet our composer's conscience shows its completeness in his obedience to the law of opera; for the music he has written to express the situations cannot be surpassed for beauty, pathos, and passion. Beethoven, like Mendelssohn, revolted from the idea of lyric drama as an art-inconsistency, but he wrote "Fidelio" to show his possibilities in a direction with which he had but little sympathy.

He composed four overtures for this opera at different periods, on account of the critical caprices of the Viennese public—a concession to public taste which his stern independence rarely made.

IV

Beethoven's relations with women were peculiar and characteristic, as were all the phases of a nature singularly self-poised and robust. Like all men of powerful imagination and keen (though perhaps not delicate) sensibility, he was strongly attracted toward the softer sex. But a certain austerity of morals, and that purity of feeling which is the inseparable shadow of one's devotion to lofty aims, always kept him within the bounds of Platonic affection. Yet there is enough in Beethoven's letters, as scanty as their indications are in this direction, to show what ardor and glow of feeling he possessed.

About the time that he was suffering keenly with the knowledge of his fast-growing infirmity, he was bound by a strong tie of affection to Countess Giulietta Guicciardi, his "immortal beloved," "his angel," "his all," "his life," as he called her in a variety of passionate utterances. It was to her that he dedicated his song "Adelaida," which as an expression of lofty passion is world-famous. Beethoven was very much dissatisfied with the work even in the glow of composition. Before the notes were dry on the music paper, the composer's old friend Barth was announced. "Here," said Beethoven, putting a roll of score paper in Earth's hands, "look at that. I have just finished it, and don't like it. There is hardly fire enough in the stove to burn it, but I will try." Barth glanced through the composition, then sang it, and soon grew into such enthusiasm as to draw from Beethoven the expression, "No? then we will not burn it, old fellow." Whether it was the reaction of disgust, which so often comes to genius after the tension of work, or whether his ideal of its lovely theme was so high as to make all effort seem inadequate, the world came very near losing what it could not afford to have missed.

The charming countess, however, preferred rank, wealth, and unruffled ease to being linked even with a great genius, if, indeed, the affair ever looked in the direction of marriage. She married another, and Beethoven does not seem to have been seriously disturbed. It may be that, like Goethe, he valued the love of woman not for itself or its direct results, but as an art-stimulus which should enrich and fructify his own intellectual life.

We get glimpses of successors to the fair countess. The beautiful Marie Pachler was for some time the object of his adoration. The affair is a somewhat mysterious one, and the lady seems to have suffered from the fire through which her powerful companion passed unscathed. Again, quaintest and oddest of all, is the fancy kindled by that "mysterious sprite of genius," as one of her contemporaries calls her, Bettina Brentano, the gifted child-woman, who fascinated all who came within her reach, from Goethe and Beethoven down to princes and nobles. Goethe's correspondence with this strange being has embalmed her life in classic literature.

Our composer's intercourse with women—for he was always alive to the charms of female society—was for the most part homely and practical in the extreme, after his deafness destroyed the zest of the more romantic phases of the divine passion. He accepted adoration, as did Dean Swift, as a right. He permitted his female admirers to knit him stockings and comforters, and make him dainty puddings and other delicacies, which he devoured with huge gusto. He condescended, in return, to go to sleep on their sofas, after picking his teeth with the candle-snuffers (so says scandal), while they thrummed away at his sonatas, the artistic slaughter of which Beethoven was mercifully unable to hear.

V

The friendship of the Archduke Rudolph relieved Beethoven of the immediate pressure of poverty; for in 1809 he settled a small life-pension upon him. The next ten years were passed by him in comparative ease and comfort, and in this time he gave to the world five of his immortal symphonies, and a large number of his finest sonatas and masses. His general health improved very much; and in his love for his nephew Karl, whom Beethoven had adopted, the lonely man found an outlet for his strong affections, which was medicine for his soul, though the object was worthless and ungrateful.

We get curious and amusing insights into the daily tenor of Beethoven's life during this period—things sometimes almost grotesque, were they not so sad. The composer lived a solitary life, and was very much at the mercy of his servants on account of his self-absorption and deafness. He was much worried by these prosaic cares. One story of a slatternly servant is as follows: The master was working at the mass in D, the great work which he commenced in 1819 for the celebration of the appointment of the Archduke Rudolph as Archbishop of Olmutz, and which should have been completed by the following year. Beethoven, however, became so engrossed with his work, and increased its proportions so much, that it was not finished until some two years after the event which it was intended to celebrate. While Beethoven was engaged upon this score, he one day woke up to the fact that some of his pages were missing. "Where on earth could they be?" he asked himself, and the servant too; but the problem remained unsolved. Beethoven, beside himself, spent hours and hours in searching, and so did the servant, but it was all in vain. At last they gave up the task as a useless one, and Beethoven, mad with despair, and pouring the very opposite to blessings upon the head of her who, he believed, was the author of the mischief, sat down with the conclusion that he must rewrite the missing part. He had no sooner commenced a new Kyrie—for this was the movement which was not to be found—than some loose sheets of score paper were discovered in the kitchen! Upon examination they proved to be the identical pages that Beethoven so much desired, and which the woman, in her anxiety to be "tidy" and to "keep things straight," had appropriated at some time or other for wrapping up, not only old boots and clothes, but also some superannuated pots and pans that were greasy and black!

Thus he was continually fretted by the carelessness or the rascality of the servants in whom he was obliged to trust. He writes in his diary: "Nancy is too uneducated for a housekeeper—indeed, quite a beast." "My precious servants were occupied from seven o'clock till ten trying to kindle a fire." "The cook's off again." "I shied half a dozen books at her head." They made his dinner so nasty he couldn't eat it. "No soup to-day, no beef, no eggs. Got something from the inn at last."

His temper and peculiarities, too, made it difficult for him to live in peace with landlords and fellow-lodgers. As his deafness increased, he struck and thumped harder at the keys of his piano, the sound of which he could scarcely hear. Nor was this all. The music that filled his brain gave him no rest. He became an inspired madman. For hours he would pace the room "howling and roaring" (as his pupil Ries puts it); or he would stand beating time with hand and foot to the music which was so vividly present to his mind. This soon put him into a feverish excitement, when, to cool himself, he would take his water-jug, and, thoughtless of everything, pour its contents over his hands, after which he could sit down to his piano. With all this it can easily be imagined that Beethoven was frequently remonstrated with. The landlord complained of a damaged ceiling, and the fellow-lodgers declared that either they or the madman must leave the house, for they could get no rest where he was. So Beethoven never for long had a resting-place. Impatient at being interfered with, he immediately packed up and went off to some other vacant lodging. From this cause he was at one time paying the rent of four lodgings at once. At times he would get tired of this changing from one place to another—from the suburbs to the town—and then he would fall back upon the hospitable home of a patron, once again taking possession of an apartment which he had vacated, probably without the least explanation or cause. One admirer of his genius, who always reserved him a chamber in his establishment, used to say to his servants: "Leave it empty; Beethoven is sure to come back again."

The instant that Beethoven entered the house he began to write and cipher on the walls, the blinds, the table, everything, in the most abstracted manner. He frequently composed on slips of paper, which he afterward misplaced, so that he had great difficulty in finding them. At one time, indeed, he forgot his own name and the date of his birth.

It is said that he once went into a Viennese restaurant, and, instead of giving an order, began to write a score on the back of the bill-of-fare, absorbed and unconscious of time and place. At last he asked how much he owed. "You owe nothing, sir," said the waiter. "What! do you think I have not dined?" "Most assuredly." "Very well, then, give me something." "What do you wish?" "Anything."

These infirmities do not belittle the man of genius, but set off his greatness as with a foil. They illustrate the thought of Goethe: "It is all the same whether one is great or small, he has to pay the reckoning of humanity."

VI

Yet beneath these eccentricities what wealth of tenderness, sympathy, and kindliness existed! His affection for his graceless nephew Karl is a touching picture. With the rest of his family he had never been on very cordial terms. His feeling of contempt for snobbery and pretense is very happily illustrated in his relations with his brother Johann. The latter had acquired property, and he sent Ludwig his card, inscribed "Johann van Beethoven, land-owner." The caustic reply was a card, on which was written, "Ludwig van Beethoven, brain-owner." But on Karl all the warmest feelings of a nature which had been starving to love and be loved poured themselves out. He gave the scapegrace every luxury and indulgence, and, self-absorbed as he was in an ideal sphere, felt the deepest interest in all the most trivial things that concerned him. Much to the uncle's sorrow, Karl cared nothing for music; but, worst of all, he was an idle, selfish, heartless fellow, who sneered at his benefactor, and valued him only for what he could get from him. At last Beethoven became fully aware of the lying ingratitude of his nephew, and he exclaims: "I know now you have no pleasure in coming to see me, which is only natural, for my atmosphere is too pure for you. God has never yet forsaken me, and no doubt some one will be found to close my eyes." Yet the generous old man forgave him, for he says in the codicil of his will, "I appoint my nephew Karl my sole heir."

Frequently, glimpses of the true vein showed themselves in such little episodes as that which occurred when Moscheles, accompanied by his brother, visited the great musician for the first time.

"Arrived at the door of the house," writes Moscheles, "I had some misgivings, knowing Beethoven's strong aversion to strangers. I therefore told my brother to wait below. After greeting Beethoven, I said: 'Will you permit me to introduce my brother to you?'

"'Where is he?' he suddenly replied.

"'Below.'

"'What, down-stairs?' and Beethoven immediately rushed off, seized hold of my brother, saying: 'Am I such a savage that you are afraid to come near me?'

"After this he showed great kindness to us."

While referring to the relations of Moscheles and Beethoven, the following anecdote related by Mme. Moscheles will be found suggestive. The pianist had been arranging some numbers of "Fidelio," which he took to the composer. He, *à la* Haydn, had inscribed the score with the words, "By God's help." Beethoven did not fail to perceive this, and he wrote underneath this phylactory the characteristic advice: "O man, help thyself."

The genial and sympathetic nature of Beethoven is illustrated in this quaint incident:

It was in the summer of 1811 that Ludwig Lowe, the actor, first met Beethoven in the dining-room of the Blue Star at Toplitz. Lowe was paying his addresses to the landlord's daughter; and conversation being impossible at the hour he dined there, the charming creature one day whispered to him: "Come at a later hour when the customers are gone and only Beethoven is here. He cannot hear, and will therefore not be in the way."

This answered for a time; but the stern parents, observing the acquaintanceship, ordered the actor to leave the house and not to return. "How great was our despair!" relates Lowe. "We both desired to correspond, but through whom? Would the solitary man at the opposite table assist us? Despite his serious reserve and seeming churlishness, I believe he is not unfriendly. I have often caught a kind smile across his bold, defiant face." Lôwe determined to try. Knowing Beethoven's custom, he contrived to meet the master when he was walking in the gardens. Beethoven instantly recognized him, and asked the reason why he no longer dined at the Blue Star. A full confession was made, and then Lowe timidly asked if he would take charge of a letter to give to the girl.

"Why not?" pleasantly observed the rough-looking musician. "You mean what is right."

So pocketing the note, he was making his way onward when Lowe again interfered.

"I beg your pardon, Herr van Beethoven, that is not all."

"So, so," said the master.

"You must also bring back the answer," Lowe went on to say.

"Meet me here at this time to-morrow," said Beethoven.

Lowe did so, and there found Beethoven awaiting him, with the coveted reply from his lady-love. In this manner Beethoven carried the letters backward and forward for some five or six weeks—in short, as long as he remained in the town.

His friendship with Ferdinand Ries commenced in a way which testified how grateful he was for kindness. When his mother lay ill at Bonn, he hurried home from Vienna just in time to witness her death. After the funeral he suffered greatly from poverty, and was relieved by Ries the violinist. Years afterward young Ries waited on Beethoven with a letter of introduction from his father. The composer received him with cordial warmth, and said: "Tell your father I have not forgotten the death of my mother." Ever afterward he was a helpful and devoted friend to young Ries, and was of inestimable value in forwarding his musical career.

Beethoven in his poverty never forgot to be generous. At a concert given in aid of wounded soldiers, where he conducted, he indignantly refused payment with the words: "Say Beethoven never accepts anything where humanity is concerned." To an Ursuline convent he gave an entirely new symphony to be performed at their benefit concert. Friend or enemy never applied to him for help that he did not freely give, even to the pinching of his own comfort.

VII

Rossini could write best when he was under the influence of Italian wine and sparkling champagne. Paesiello liked the warm bed in which to jot down his musical notions, and we are told that "it was between the sheets that he planned the 'Barber of Seville,' the 'Molinara,' and so many other *chefs-d'oeuvre* of ease and gracefulness." Mozart could chat and play at billiards or bowls at the same time that he composed the most beautiful music. Sacchini found it impossible to write anything of any beauty unless a pretty woman was by his side, and he was surrounded by his cats, whose graceful antics stimulated and affected him in a marked fashion. "Gluck," Bombet says, "in order to warm his imagination and to transport himself to Aulis or Sparta, was accustomed to place himself in the middle of a beautiful meadow. In this situation, with his piano before him, and a bottle of champagne on each side, he wrote in the open air his two 'Iphigenias,' his 'Orpheus,' and some other works." The agencies which stimulated Beethoven's grandest thoughts are eminently characteristic of the man. He loved to let the winds and storms beat on his bare head, and see the dazzling play of the lightning. Or, failing the sublimer moods of Nature, it was his delight to walk in the woods and fields, and take in at every pore the influences which she so lavishly bestows on her favorites. His true life was his ideal life in art. To him it was a mission and an inspiration, the end and object of all things; for these had value only as they fed the divine craving within.

"Nothing can be more sublime," he writes, "than to draw nearer to the Godhead than other men, and to diffuse here on earth these Godlike rays among mortals." Again: "What is all this compared to the grandest of all Masters of Harmony— above, above?"

> "All experience seemed an arch, wherethrough
> Gleamed that untraveled world, whose margin fades
> Forever and forever as we move."

The last four years of our composer's life were passed amid great distress from poverty and feebleness. He could compose but little; and, though his friends solaced his latter days with attention and kindness, his sturdy independence would not accept more. It is a touching fact that Beethoven voluntarily suffered want and privation in his last years, that he might leave the more to his selfish and ungrateful nephew. He died in 1827, in his fifty-seventh year, and is buried in the Wahring Cemetery near Vienna. Let these extracts from a testamentary paper addressed to his brothers in 1802, in expectation of death, speak more eloquently of the hidden life of a heroic soul than any other words could:

> "O ye, who consider or declare me to be hostile, obstinate,
> or misanthropic, what injustice ye do me! Ye know not
> the secret causes of that which to you wears such an
> appearance. My heart and my mind were from childhood
> prone to the tender feelings of affection. Nay, I was
> always disposed even to perform great actions. But, only
> consider that, for the last six years, I have been attacked
> by an incurable complaint, aggravated by the unskillful
> treatment of medical men, disappointed from year to year

in the hope of relief, and at last obliged to submit to the endurance of an evil the cure of which may last perhaps for years, if it is practicable at all. Born with a lively, ardent disposition, susceptible to to the diversions of society, I was forced at an early age to renounce them, and to pass my life in seclusion. If I strove at any time to set myself above all this, oh how cruelly was I driven back by the doubly painful experience of my defective hearing! and yet it was not possible for me to say to people, 'Speak louder—bawl—for I am deaf!' Ah! how could I proclaim the defect of a sense that I once possessed in the highest perfection—in a perfection in which few of my colleagues possess or ever did possess it? Indeed, I cannot! Forgive me, then, if ye see me draw back when I would gladly mingle among you. Doubly mortifying is my misfortune to me, as it must tend to cause me to be misconceived. From recreation in the society of my fellow-creatures, from the pleasures of conversation, from the effusions of friendship, I am cut off. Almost alone in the world, I dare not venture into society more than absolute necessity requires. I am obliged to live as an exile. If I go into company, a painful anxiety comes over me, since I am apprehensive of being exposed to the danger of betraying my situation. Such has been my state, too, during this half year that I have spent in the country. Enjoined by my intelligent physician to spare my hearing as much as possible, I have been almost encouraged by him in my present natural disposition, though, hurried away by my fondness for society, I sometimes suffered myself to be enticed into it. But what a humiliation when any one standing beside me could hear at a distance a flute that I could not hear, or any one heard the shepherd singing, and I could not distinguish a sound! Such circumstances brought me to the brink of despair, and had well-nigh made me put an end to my life: nothing but my art held my hand. Ah! it seemed to me impossible to quit the world before I had produced all that I felt myself called to accomplish. And so I endured this wretched life—so truly wretched, that a somewhat speedy change is capable of transporting me from the best into the worst condition. Patience—so I am told—I must choose for my guide. Steadfast, I hope, will be my resolution to persevere, till it shall please the inexorable Fates to cut the thread. Perhaps there may be an amendment—perhaps not; I am prepared for the worst—I, who so early as my twenty-eighth year was forced to become a philosopher—it is not easy—for the artist more difficult than for any other. O God! thou lookest down upon my misery; thou knowest that it is accompanied with love of my fellow-creatures, and a disposition to do good! O men! when ye shall read this, think that ye have wronged me; and let the child of affliction take comfort on finding one like himself, who, in spite of all the impediments of Nature, yet did all that lay in his power to obtain admittance into the rank of worthy artists and men.... I go to meet death with joy. If he comes before I have had occasion to develop all my professional abilities, he will come too soon for me, in spite of my hard fate, and I should wish that he had delayed his arrival. But even then I am content, for he will release me from a state of endless suffering. Come when thou wilt, I shall meet thee with firmness. Farewell, and do not quite forget me after I am dead; I have deserved that you should think of me, for in my lifetime I have often thought of you to make you happy. May you ever be so!"

VIII

The music of Beethoven has left a profound impress on art. In speaking of his genius it is difficult to keep expression within the limits of good taste. For who has so passed into the very inner *penetralia* of his great art, and revealed to the world such heights and depths of beauty and power in sound?

Beethoven composed nine symphonies, which, by one voice, are ranked as the greatest ever written, reaching in the last, known as the "Choral," the full perfection of his power and experience. Other musicians have composed symphonic works remarkable for varied excellences, but in Beethoven this form of writing seems to have attained its highest possibilities, and to have been illustrated by the greatest variety of effects, from the sublime to such as are simply beautiful and melodious. His hand swept the whole range of expression with unfaltering mastery. Some passages may seem obscure, some too elaborately wrought, some startling and abrupt, but on all is stamped the die of his great genius.

Beethoven's compositions for the piano, the sonatas, are no less notable for range and power of expression, their adaptation to meet all the varied moods of passion and sentiment. Other pianoforte composers have given us more warm and vivid color, richer sensual effects of tone, more wild and bizarre combination, perhaps even greater sweetness in melody; but we look in vain elsewhere for the spiritual passion and poetry, the aspiration and longing, the lofty humanity, which make the Beethoven sonatas the *suspiria de pro-fundis* of the composer's inner life. In addition to his symphonies and sonatas, he wrote the great opera of "Fidelio," and in the field of oratorio asserted his equality with Handel and Haydn by composing "The Mount of Olives." A great variety of chamber music, masses, and songs, bear the same imprint of power. He may be called the most original and conscientious of all the composers. Handel, Haydn, Mozart, Schubert, and Mendelssohn were inveterate thieves, and pilfered the choicest gems from old and forgotten writers without scruple. Beethoven seems to have been so fecund in great conceptions, so lifted on the wings of his tireless genius, so austere in artistic morality, that he stands for the most part above the reproach deservedly borne by his brother composers. Beethoven's principal title to fame is in his superlative place as a symphonic composer. In the symphony music finds its highest intellectual dignity; in Beethoven the symphony has found its loftiest master.

A Chapter from
The Great German Composers, 1878

ON HEARING A
SYMPHONY OF BEETHOVEN

By Edna St. Vincent Millay

Sweet sounds, oh, beautiful music, do not cease!
Reject me not into the world again.
With you alone is excellence and peace,
Mankind made plausible, his purpose plain.
Enchanted in your air benign and shrewd,
With limbs a-sprawl and empty faces pale,
The spiteful and the stingy and the rude
Sleep like the scullions in the fairy-tale.
This moment is the best the world can give:
The tranquil blossom on the tortured stem.
Reject me not, sweet sounds; oh, let me live,
Till Doom espy my towers and scatter them,
A city spell-bound under the aging sun.
Music my rampart, and my only one.

A Poem from
The Buck in the Snow, 1928

Ludwig Van Beethoven

LUDWIG VAN BEETHOVEN

By Kathrine Lois Scobey & Olive Brown Horne

EARLY LIFE OF BEETHOVEN

Some day you may be fortunate enough to cross the broad Atlantic and visit European countries. If you are, you will surely wish to go to Germany. Many hundreds of travellers go there every year to take a trip down the Rhine. It is said to be the most beautiful river in all the world.

There are many interesting things to be seen on a trip down the Rhine. On one side green vineyards slope down to the river. On the other side rocky bluffs rise abruptly from the water's edge. Old castles stand on many of the bluffs. Some of the castles are in ruins and are almost hidden by the overgrowing ivy.

Many are the cities and villages that have been built along the banks of the Rhine. Some of the cities are quaint and old-fashioned. Bonn is such a city. The people of Bonn are very proud of a certain low building that faces a narrow street. They take every traveler to see it. They point over the door to a tablet on which are carved words meaning, "In this house Ludwig van Beethoven was born, December 17, 1770."

Ludwig van Beethoven was one of the great German composers. In fact, many people consider him the greatest composer that the world has ever known. Whether this be true or not, certain it is that his music is loved in every land. Nearly a century and a half has passed since Ludwig van Beethoven was born in his humble home in Bonn. Ludwig's father was a singer. He was a good-for-nothing sort of fellow. He never earned

57

enough money to support his family well.

He was paid about one hundred and twenty-five dollars a year for singing in a church. Besides this he made money by giving music lessons. He spent the little money that he had carelessly. He often spent it for himself when it was greatly needed by his wife and children.

Indeed, if it had not been for the good old grandfather, things would have gone hard with the Beethoven family. As long as he lived, he was a great help to them in every way. There were several Beethoven children, but Ludwig was his grandfather's pet and was named for him.

Ludwig was only three years old when his grandfather died. Well did the boy remember the old gentleman's scarlet coat and flashing eye. Well did he remember, too, his love and kindness.

The mother of the great Beethoven was a patient, hard-working woman. He never forgot the lessons of truth and obedience he received from her. Beethoven always spoke tenderly of his mother and never forgot her patience. When he was a young man, he wrote, "She was a dear, good mother and my best friend."

Little Ludwig was hardly out of his cradle before his father gave him music lessons. While he was still a tiny lad, he was compelled to practice many hours each day. When he was only four years old, the neighbors often saw him sitting on a bench by the door, sobbing. He cried because he knew that he must soon go in to work at his scales.

Ludwig's father hoped that his son would learn music rapidly. He wished to have him play in concerts as Mozart had done when a boy. He thought that in this way much money might be earned. So he kept the lad almost constantly at work at his music. Ludwig practiced almost all the time when he was not at school or sleeping.

The boy studied two instruments, the piano and the violin. At first his father was his only teacher. But soon a regular music teacher was employed. The boy practiced hours at a time. When we think how much work was required of the little fellow, we almost wonder that he did not hate his music. But this was not the case. On the contrary, he liked it better than anything else in the wide world.

By the time Ludwig van Beethoven was ten years old, he had become a fine organist. He had received some lessons on the organ. His teacher was organist in the prince's chapel. Once upon a time this man was called away from Bonn. Wondering whom he could get to play in his absence, he thought and thought. Finally he said: "Perhaps the boy, Beethoven, could take my place. I will give him the chance, and we shall see what the lad can do."

How proud was the boy when his teacher honored him in this way! He said to himself: "I must do my very best. I do not want my master to be ashamed of his pupil." He put forth his best efforts, and every one who heard him had words of praise for his playing. When the master returned and heard of it, he said, "Some day this boy will be as famous as Mozart."

The organist in the chapel at Bonn did not know how true his words were. He did not dream that one day the German people would be proud to erect a monument in Bonn to this same Beethoven. Little did he imagine that the one word *Beethoven* would be considered sufficient to carve at the base of the monument.

With the other Beethoven children, Ludwig was sent to school. He had lessons in all the common school studies and in French, Latin, and Italian besides.

Early in his teens, Ludwig was appointed second court organist. He was paid for this work, but the knowledge of great composers which he gained was worth more to him than the money he received.

Although in after years Beethoven was untidy, he cared much for dress when he was court organist. Every one turned to look at the little fellow in his sea-green coat and white flowered waistcoat. With his hat under his arm and with his sword at his side, young Beethoven looked very much like one of the gentlemen of the court.

BEETHOVEN IN VIENNA

The year 1787 was one which Beethoven never forgot. That was the year in which he first went to Vienna. He was at that time seventeen years old. For many months he had been longing to visit the Austrian capital.

For a long time Beethoven had been saving his money to take this trip. Like all other young musicians of those days, he had a great desire to study in Vienna. He hoped, too, that he should be fortunate enough to play for Mozart. In this he was not disappointed.

You may imagine how happy Beethoven must have been to meet Mozart one day and to be allowed to play for him. He played selections from the great composers, until Mozart said: "Many others can do what you have just done. I have heard that you often compose as you play. Sit down again and compose for me."

The young musician was excited, but he was not afraid. He knew that he should succeed. He had often composed as he played, and felt sure that he could do it now. For a few moments only there was silence. Then the boy's fingers moved swiftly over the keys, and the room was filled with the sweetest music. Not once did the lad falter, not once did he make the slightest mistake.

Mozart was astonished. He was amazed that this German boy showed such skill. He listened for a while in silence; then he arose and tiptoed from the room. He whispered to some friends, "Keep your eye on this youth. He will make a noise in the world some day."

Beethoven had been in Vienna only a short time when he received sad news from home.

Beethoven at the House of Mozart
By H. Merle

A letter from Bonn told him that his mother was dying. He hastened home, and reached there only a few days before her death.

Beethoven was very sad. He wrote to a friend, "Who was happier than I so long as I could speak the sweet name of mother? There is none to whom I can say it now."

Beethoven decided to remain in Bonn. He felt that he must do something to help support the family; so he made up his mind to give music lessons.

Among his pupils was a lad from one of the wealthiest families of Bonn. The mother in this family was a woman of culture and refinement. She often invited Beethoven to her home and talked with him as his own mother might have done.

She gave him the finest books to read. He became interested

in the best writings. He read the poems of Goethe with great pleasure, and was fond of English poets as well. He spent many hours studying the works of Shakespeare and Milton.

For five years Beethoven taught music in his native town. During this time he made many friends. One of these was a count, and a very good friend he proved to be.

After Beethoven's first visit to Vienna he longed to go there again. His friend, the count, had often heard him express this wish. The gift of a piano and some money from the count helped Beethoven to obtain his wish.

In 1792 he went to Vienna to study music. He became the pupil of Haydn. He did not have many lessons from that teacher, for Haydn soon left the city.

When Mozart was twenty-five he had published nearly three hundred compositions. Beethoven at the same age had published almost none. After his arrival in Vienna, however, he began to write down some of the beautiful music which filled his mind. These compositions won for him many friends among the families of rank in Vienna.

Princes and nobles vied with one another in entertaining him. They saw in him a musician of great promise. They were proud that such a composer had chosen Vienna for his home. They appreciated his music and were always glad to hear it.

Scarcely a day passed that Beethoven did not play in the home of some person of wealth. During the first few years that he spent in Vienna, he did not appear in concerts. He played only in the homes of his friends, where his symphonies delighted all hearers.

Beethoven was an eccentric man. His friends were people of fashion, but he cared little for style. In fact, he was often untidy in his dress. His clothes were loose and ill-fitting. His hair was long and unkempt.

Beethoven in his Study
By C. Schloesser

His aristocratic friends were polished and courteous in their manners. Beethoven was impolite and even rude at times.

In spite of all these faults, his friends were fond of Beethoven. It has been said of him, that he "never let go of what seemed to him the right." He was honest and sincere in all that he did. He was warm-hearted and generous. For all these things he was loved.

Among Beethoven's friends was a prince. He and his wife lived in a beautiful palace and kept many servants. They invited Beethoven to live with them. He was a member of their household for several years.

The prince had four musicians in his home. These men played together to entertain the prince, the princess, and their friends. Beethoven devoted much time to the training of these musicians. He spent many hours in teaching them the works of the famous composers.

Those years in Vienna were filled with hard work for Beethoven. He learned to play upon many instruments. He studied the horn, viola, violin, and clarinet. He did this that he might know better how to write music for the orchestra.

The citizens of Vienna were a music-loving people. Many of them had never had an opportunity of hearing Beethoven play. They were anxious to listen to some of his own compositions; but he did not like to play before a large audience. At last he appeared in public. In 1795 he gave several concerts. One of these was for the benefit of Mozart's widow and children.

When Beethoven was about thirty years old, a sad misfortune befell him. He realized that he was becoming deaf. He tried the best doctors, but they could do nothing for him. His deafness slowly increased.

When the musician first knew of his deafness, he told no one. He seldom went to the homes of his friends, for he could not bear to have them know that he was deaf.

Beethoven was never happier than when he was in the country. He spent all his summers there. Every day he wandered for hours through the woods. When he became deaf, he wrote to a friend, "It makes me sad to think that others can hear the notes of a far-off flute or a distant shepherd's song, and I can not."

To another friend he wrote: "My deafness troubles me less here than elsewhere. Every tree seems to speak to me of God. How happy am I to wander through the cool paths of the forest! No one can love the country as I do!"

Even though he was deaf, Beethoven sometimes tried to lead the orchestra. One time a symphony of his was played at a concert. Every seat in the large hall was filled. Beethoven took his place, and at a signal from him the music began. It was the Ninth Symphony. The people listened in silence to the beautiful music. When the last note had died away, the room was perfectly quiet for a moment. Then a storm of applause broke forth.

Beethoven, with his back to the people, did not hear it. He knew not that his symphony had so greatly pleased them. The clapping grew louder and louder. Then one of the musicians touched Beethoven upon the arm. He turned and saw what he had not been able to hear. As the deaf musician bowed, the eyes of many were filled with tears.

Beethoven often went to the park when he wished to write. There, in the thickest part of the wood, some of his most beautiful music was composed. He sat in the fork of an old oak and wrote, sometimes a symphony, sometimes a sonata.

The master was once invited to try a new organ in a large monastery. A few friends went with him. When they arrived, the chapel was almost empty. No one could be seen except a few monks at their prayers and some peasants sweeping out the long aisles.

Beethoven went at once to the great organ. At first the music was soft and sweet. Gradually the tones grew richer and fuller. The music rose and fell until the beautiful tones were echoed from every corner of the shadowy chapel.

Little by little, the church, at first so empty, became filled with groups of black-gowned monks. Beethoven had no thought of the silent, listening people and they had no thought of him. The heavenly music had turned their thoughts to God. The lips of the monks moved in prayer, and the peasants, before so busy, had dropped their brooms and were standing with folded hands and bowed heads.

Beethoven was a hard worker. Strange to say, the greater part of his work was done after he became deaf. He often rose at three in the morning to write a concerto or a symphony. Sometimes he worked far into the night, composing a sonata or a serenade. His published works number several hundred pieces of music.

The last years of the great master's life were sad. For a long time he had been unable to hear the notes of his loved piano. "He, the maker of sweet sounds, could not hear his own voice, or catch the words that fell from the lips of those he loved."

During his last illness Beethoven found great comfort in reading music. A friend sent him some of Haydn's compositions. Beethoven passed many pleasant hours reading them. He found much comfort, too, in Schubert's *Songs*.

Beethoven died in 1827. A few days before his death he said, "I shall soon go upon the long journey." His last words were, "I shall hear in heaven."

THE MOONLIGHT SONATA
(Adapted)

It happened at Vienna. One moonlight evening, in early summer, a friend called upon Beethoven. He said, "Come, let us walk together in the moonlight." Arm in arm the two friends strolled through the city. In passing through a dark, narrow street, Beethoven paused suddenly. "Hush!" he said. "What sound is that? It is from my sonata in F. Hark, how well it is played!"

It was a mean little dwelling before which the two friends paused to listen. The music went on. Almost at the end of the beautiful sonata, the music ceased, and low sobs were heard instead. A girl's soft voice said, "I can go no farther. It is too beautiful. I have not the power to play it as it should be played. Oh, what would I not give to go to one of Beethoven's concerts!"

"Ah, my sister," said another voice, "why wish for that which you can not have? We can scarcely pay our rent."

"You are right," answered the girl, "and yet I wish for once in my life to hear some really good music."

"Such a wish will never be granted," said her companion.

Beethoven looked at his friend. "Let us go in," he said.

"Go in! Why should we go in?"

"I will play for her," said the master, in a low tone. "This girl has the soul of a musician. I will play for her, and she will understand." Without waiting for an answer his hand was upon the door.

As the two friends entered the room, they saw a pale young man sitting by a table making shoes. Near him sat a young girl. She was leaning sorrowfully upon an old-fashioned harpsichord. Her long golden hair fell over her neck and shoulders. Both the young man and the girl were very poorly dressed. Both started and turned toward the door as the strangers entered the room.

"Pardon me," said Beethoven, "but I heard the music and was tempted to enter. I am a musician."

The girl blushed, and the young man appeared annoyed. "I also heard something of what you said," continued Beethoven. "Shall I play for you? Shall I give you a concert?"

Beethoven's manner was so friendly and his voice so kindly that a smile took the place of the frown on the young man's face. The four, who but a moment ago were strangers, became friends at once.

"Thank you," said the shoemaker, "but our harpsichord is so poor and we have no music."

"No music," echoed Beethoven. "How then does the young lady play so—" He stopped suddenly, for the girl turned her face toward him, and for the first time he saw that she was blind.

"I beg your pardon," he stammered, "but I had not noticed before. Then you play by ear?"

"Yes, entirely," the girl answered.

"And where do you hear music, since you attend no concerts?" asked Beethoven.

"I used to hear a lady practicing near us. During the summer evenings her windows were often open, and I walked to and fro outside to listen."

The girl seemed shy, so Beethoven said no more. He seated himself quietly before the harpsichord and began to play. Never before had Beethoven played as he played that night for the blind girl and her brother. From the moment that his fingers began to wander over the keys, the very tone of the instrument seemed to grow sweeter.

The brother and sister were silent with wonder. The young man laid aside his work, and the girl sat perfectly quiet. She leaned forward a little as if afraid lest she might miss a single note of the sweet music.

Suddenly the flame of the one candle wavered, sank, flickered, and went out. Beethoven paused. His friend rose quietly and threw open the shutters. A flood of soft moonlight filled the room, so that it was almost as light as before. The moonbeams fell brightest upon the piano and the player.

But the music had stopped. The master's head dropped upon his breast, and his hands rested upon his knees. He seemed lost in thought, and sat thus for some time.

At length the young shoemaker arose. Eagerly, yet timidly, he approached the musician. "Wonderful man!" he said in a low tone, "who art thou?"

One of the composer's rare smiles flitted across his face. "Listen!" he said, and with a master's touch he gave the opening bars of his own sonata in F.

The girl seemed to know that no one but the composer of the music could have played it so well. "Then you are Beethoven," she exclaimed. Beethoven rose to go, but they begged him to stay. "Play to us once more—only once more."

He again seated himself at the piano. The moon shone brightly through the window. Looking up thoughtfully to the sky and stars, he said, "I will compose a sonata to the moonlight." Touching the keys lightly, he began to play a sad and lovely melody. The music filled the room as gently as the soft moonlight creeps over the dark earth.

Then the time changed. The music became brighter and more rapid. One no longer seemed to see the moon gliding through fleecy clouds. Instead, one thought of sprites and fairies dancing merrily together.

Once again the music changed. The notes were as rapid as before, but they seemed fraught with sadness. It was such music as fills the heart with wonder.

"Farewell to you," said Beethoven, pushing back his chair and turning toward the door. "Farewell to you."

"You will come again?" said the brother and sister in one breath.

He paused and looked tenderly at the face of the blind girl. "Yes, yes," he said, "I will come again and give you some lessons. Farewell! I will come soon again." His new friends followed him in silence and stood at the door until he was out of sight and hearing.

"Let us hasten home," said Beethoven to his friend. "I must write out that sonata while the music is still in my mind." When they reached home, Beethoven seated himself at once and began to write. He worked until daybreak. When he had finished, he had written the *Moonlight Sonata*.

A Chapter from
Stories of Great Musicians, 1905

Ludwig Van Beethoven

BEETHOVEN

THE GREAT BUMBLEBEE

By Rupert Hughes

"No artist has ever penetrated further, for none has ever thrust the thorn of life deeper into his own heart, and won, by the surrender of it, his success and his immortality."

So says the profuse Ludwig Nohl in his reprint of the diary of a young Spanish-Italian woman, Fanny Giannatasio del Rio, who knew Beethoven well and loved him well, and as mutely as "a violet blooming at his feet in utter disregard."

Beethoven the man would be voted altogether impossible either as friend or as lover, if he had not had so marvellous, so compulsive, a genius. He was short, pock-marked, ugly, slovenly, surly to the point of ferocity, whimsical to the brink of mania, egotistic to the environs of self-idolatry, diseased and deaf, embittered, morose—all the brutal epithets you wish to hurl at him. But withal he had the majesty of a Prometheus chained to the rocks; like Prometheus, he had stolen the very fires of heaven; like Prometheus, he did not suffer in silence, but roared or moaned his demigodlike anguishes in immortal rhythms.

A strange contrast he made with the versatile, the catholic, the elegant and cheerful Goethe, his acquaintance, and his rival in collecting women's loves into an encyclopaedic emotional life.

Beethoven, unlike his fellow giant Händel, despised the pleasures of the table; he substituted a passion for nature. "No man on earth can love the country as I do!" he wrote; and proved it in his life. His mother died when he was young, and he found a foster-mother in Frau von Breuning, of Bonn. Her daughter Eleonore, nicknamed "Lorchen," seems to have won his heart awhile; she knitted him an Angola waistcoat and a neckcloth, which brought tears to his eyes; they spatted, and he wrote her two humbly affectionate notes which you may read with much other intimate matter in the two volumes of his published letters. He still had her silhouette in 1826, when he was fifty-six.

Three years before, he had succumbed, at the age of twenty, to the charms of Barbara Koch, the daughter of a widow who kept the café where Beethoven ate; she made it almost a salon of intellectual conversation. Barbara later became a governess in the family of Count von Belderbusch, whom eventually she married. Next was the highborn blonde and coquettish Jeannette d'Honrath, who used to tease him by singing ironical love ditties. Then came Fräulein Westerhold, whom he loved vainly in the Wertherlike fashion.

Doctor Wegeler, who married Eleonore von Breuning, said that "In Vienna, at all events while I was there, from 1794 to 1796, Beethoven was always in love with some one, and very often succeeded in making a conquest where many an Adonis would have found it most difficult to gain a hearing. I will also call attention to the fact that, so far as I know, each of Beethoven's beloved ones was of high rank."

To continue the catalogue. There is a picture extant of a Cupid singeing Psyche's wings with a torch; it is inscribed: "A New Year's gift for the tantalising Countess Charlotte von Brunswick, from her friend, Beethoven."

There was Magdalena Willmann, a singer, whom he as a youth befriended and proposed to in later days, only to be refused, "because he was very ugly and half crazy," as she told her niece.

An army captain cut him out with Fräulein d'Honrath; his

good friend Stephan von Breuning won away from him the "schöne und hochgebildete" Julie von Vering, whom Beethoven loved and by whom he was encouraged; she married Stephan in 1808, and died eleven months later, after Beethoven had dedicated to her part of a concerto. He wrote a letter beautiful with sympathy to poor Stephan. Then he loved Fräulein Thérèse von Malfatti and begged her in vain to marry him. He called her the "volatile Thérèse who takes life so lightly." She married the Baron von Droszdick. We have a letter wherein Beethoven says: "Farewell, my dearest Thérèse; I wish you all the good and charm that life can offer. Think of me kindly, and forget my follies." She had a cousin Mathilde—later the Baroness Gleichenstein—who also left a barb in the well-smitten and accessible target of his heart. Even Hummel, the pianist, was his successful rival in a love affair with Fräulein Roeckel.

The Hungarian Countess Marie Erdödy (née Countess Niczky) is listed among his flames, though Schindler thinks it "nothing more than a friendly intimacy between the two." Still, she gave Beethoven an apartment in her house in 1809, and he writes that she had paid a servant extra money to stay with him—a task servants always required bribing to achieve. But Thayer says that such a ménage could not last, as Beethoven was "too irritable, too freakish and too stubborn, too easily injured and too hardly reconciled." Beethoven dedicated to her certain trios, and she erected in one of her parks in Hungary a handsome temple in his honour, with an inscription of homage to him. In his letters he calls her his "confessor," and in one he addresses her as "Liebe, liebe, liebe, liebe Gräfin," showing that she was his dearie to the fourth power.

Also there was Amalie Sebald, "a nut-brown maid of Berlin," a twenty-five-year-old singer, of beauty and brain. In a letter to Tiedge in 1812, Beethoven says:

"Two affectionate words for a farewell would have sufficed me; alas! not even one was said to me! The Countess

73

von der Recke sends me a pressure of the hand; it is something, and I kiss her hands as a token of gratitude; but Amalie has not even saluted me. Every day I am angry at myself in not having profited by her sojourn at Teplitz, seeking her companionship sooner. It is a frightful thing to make the acquaintance of such a sweet creature, and to lose her immediately; and nothing is more insupportable than thus to have to confess one's own foolishness.... Be happy, if suffering humanity can be. Give, on my part, to the countess a cordial but respectful pressure of the hand, and to Amalie a right ardent kiss—if nobody there can see."

In Nohl's collection of Beethoven's letters is an inscription in the album of the singer, Mine. "Auguste" Sebald (a mistake for "Amalie"). The inscription reads, as Lady Wallace ungrammatically Englishes it:

"Ludwig van Beethoven:
Who even if you would
Forget you never should."

In another work, Nohl mentions the existence of a mass of short notes from Beethoven to her, showing "not so much the warm, effervescent passion of youth, as the deep, quieter sentiment of personal esteem and affection, which comes later in life, and, in consequence, is much more lasting." One of the letters he quotes. It runs:

"What are you dreaming about, saying that you can be nothing to me? We will talk this over by word of mouth. I am ever wishing that my presence may bring peace and rest to you, and that you could have confidence in me. I shall hope to be better to-morrow, and that we shall be able to pass a few hours together in the enjoyment of nature while you remain here. Good night, dear Amalie; many, many thanks for the proof you give me of your attachment to your friend,

"BEETHOVEN."

There are other of these notes in Thayer's biography. She seems to have called the composer "a tyrant," and he has much playfulness of allusion to the idea, and there is much about the wretchedness of his health. Amalie Sebald seems to have been of great solace to him, but, like all the rest, she married some one else, Justice-councillor Krause.

It was for her that Beethoven composed his cycle of songs, "To the far-away love" [An die ferne Geliebte], according to Thayer; and of her that he wrote to Ries: "All good wishes to your wife. I, alas, have none; I have found but one, and her I can never possess."

Years later he said to his friend Giannatasio that five years before he had loved unhappily; he would have considered marriage the happiness of his life, but it was "not to be thought of for a moment, almost an utter impracticability, a chimera." Still, he said, his love was as strong as ever; he had never found such harmony, and, though he never proposed, he could never get her out of his mind.

In 1812 Carl Maria von Weber was in Berlin, and became ever after a devoted admirer of Amalie's virtues, her intellect, and her beauty.

Five years later we learn of Beethoven's receiving letters and presents from "a Bremen maiden," a pianist, Elise Müller. And there was a poetess who also annoyed him.

In this same year, 1817, he was much in the society of "the beautiful and amiable" Frau Marie L. Pachler-Koschak, of Gratz. He had met her in 1812, and admired her playing. As late as 1826 we have letters from her, inviting him to visit her in Gratz.

Bettina Brentano von Arnim

But in 1817—he being then forty-seven years old—the acquaintance was so cordial that Schindler, who observed it, called it an "autumnal love," though the woman's son later asserted that it was only a kinship of "artistic sympathy,"—in fact, Beethoven called her "a true foster-mother to the creations of his brain." Thayer says, however, that Beethoven never met her till after she married. Beethoven is implicated in the riddle of the letters of Bettina Brentano von Arnim. This freakish young woman had some acquaintance with Goethe, and after his death published letters alleged to have been sent to her by him. She also gave the world certain letters said to have come to her from Beethoven. It has been pretty well proved that the naive Bettina was an ardent and painstaking forger on a large scale. She included a series of sonnets which were written to another of Goethe's "garden of girls" before he ever met Bettina. But she appears to have vitiated her clever forgeries by a certain alloy of truth, and it may be that her Beethoven letters are, after all, fictions founded on fact. The language of these letters is somewhat overstrained, but Beethoven could rant on occasion, and Ludwig Nohl believed the letters to be genuine, since a friend of his said he had seen them and recognised Beethoven's script. Thayer accepts the entanglement with Bettina as a fact, and thinks it was, at that crisis in Beethoven's life, "a happy circumstance that Bettina Brentano came, with her beauty, her charm, and her spirit, to lead his thoughts in other paths."

Wegeler has alluded to the fact that Beethoven's love affairs were always with women of high degree. But others have called him a "promiscuous lover," because he once used to stare amorously at a handsome peasant girl and watch her labouring in the garden, only to be mocked by her; and more especially because of a memorandum of his pupil Ries, who wrote: "Beethoven never visited me more frequently than when I lived in the house of a tailor with three very handsome but thoroughly respectable daughters." In 1804 Beethoven wrote him a twitting allusion to these girls. But such a flirtation means little, and besides they were beauties, these daughters of the tailor. And Beethoven's own mother was a cook.

Ries describes him as a sad flirt. "Beethoven had a great liking for female society, especially young and beautiful girls, and often when we met out-of-doors a charming face, he would turn round, put up his glass, and gaze eagerly at her, and then smile and nod if he found I was observing him. He was always falling in love with some one, but generally his passion did not last long. Once when I teased him on his conquest of a very beautiful woman, he confessed that she had enchanted him longest, and most seriously of all—namely, seven whole months!"

Ries also records a humourous scandal of an occasion when he found Beethoven flirting desperately with a fair unknown; Ries sat down at the piano and improvised incidental music to Beethoven's directions— *"amoroso," "a malinconico"* and the like.

Once a devoted admirer, wife of a Vienna pianist, longed for a lock of the composer's outrageously unkempt hair, and asked a friend to get her one. At his suggestion, Beethoven, who was a practical joker of boorish capabilities, sent her a tuft from the chin of a goat. The trick was discovered, and the scorned woman vented her fury in a letter; the repentant Beethoven made ample apology to her, and spent his wrath on the head of the suggester of the mischief.

Crowest spins a pretty yarn of Beethoven's acting as *"postillon d'amour"* by carrying love letters for a clandestinely loving couple.

Many of his own love-longings were couched in the form of the dedications prefixed to his compositions. The piano sonata, Op. 7, was inscribed to the Countess Babette von Keglevics, later the Princess Odeschalchi, and is called for her sake "der Verliebte." Other "gewidmets" were to the Princesses Lichtenstein and von Kinsky, to the Countesses von Browne, Lichnowsky, von Clary, von Erdödy, von Brunswick, Wolf-Metternich, the Baroness Ertmann (his "liebe, werthe, Dorothea Cäcilia"), and to Eleonora von Breuning.

All these make a fairly good bead-roll of love-affairs for a busy, ugly, and half-savage man. It is not so long as Leporello's list of Don Juan's conquests, "but, marry, t'will do, t'will serve." I find I have catalogued twenty-six thus far (counting the tailor's three daughters as one). And more are to come.

And yet, in the face of such a directory of desire, you'll find Von Seyfried and Haslinger venturing the statement, that "Beethoven was never married, and, what was more marvellous still, never had any love passages in his life," while Francis Hueffer can speak of "his grand, chaste way." On this latter point there is room for debate. Crowest adopts both sides at once by saying: "In the main, authorities concur in Beethoven's attachments being always honourable. There can be no doubt, however, that he was an impetuous suitor, ready to continue an acquaintance into a more serious bond on the slenderest ground, and without the slightest regard to the consequences on either side." Thayer takes a middle ground,—that, in the Vienna of his time and his social grade, it was impossible that Beethoven should have been a Puritan, while he was, however, a man of distinctly clean mind. He could not endure loose talk, and he once boxed the ears of a barmaid who teased him. All his life he had a horror of intrigue with another man's wife, and he once snubbed a man who conducted such an affair.

Why, then, thus warm-hearted and clean-hearted, thus woman-loving, did he never marry? Ah, here is one of the sombrest tragedies of art. To say, "Poor Beethoven!" is like pitying the sick lion in his lair. Yet what is more pitiful? Love was the thorn in this lion's flesh, and there was no Fräulein Androcles to take it away.

Beethoven was born to the humblest station and the haughtiest aspirations, was left to a sot and a slave-driver for a father, and was early orphaned of his mother. In the first letter we have of his, he says: "She was a good and tender mother to me; she was my best friend. Ah, who was more happy than I when I could still breathe the sweet name of 'mother!' to ears that heard? Whom now can I say it to? Only to the mute image of her that my fancy paints."

This same letter, written when he was seventeen, tells three other of his life-long griefs—lack of funds, ill health, and melancholia. He had no childhood; his salad days were bitter herbs; his later life was one wild tempest of ambition frustrated, of love unsated or unreturned, of friendship misprized or thought to be misprized.

And then his deafness! When he was only thirty, the black fog of silence began to sink across his life; two years later he was stone-deaf, and nearly half his days were spent in the dungeon of isolation from real communion with man or with his own great music. He lived, indeed, as he said, *inter lacrimas et luctum.*

The blind are usually placid and trustful; it is the major affliction of the deaf that they grow suspicious of their intimates and abhorrent of themselves. There is nothing in history more majestic than the battle of this giant soul against his doom; nothing more heartrending than his bitter outcries; nothing loftier than his high determination to serve his turn on earth in spite of all. He was the very King Lear of music, trudging his lonely way with heart broken and hair wild in the storms that buffeted him vainly toward the cliffs of self-destruction.

To such a man a home was a refuge pitifully needed, and for a while longingly sought. I have mentioned various women to whom he offered the glorious martyrdom that a life with him must needs have been. There were two others whom he deeply loved. One of these was the famous Italienne, whose very name is honey and romance as he writes it in the dedication of his "Moonlight Sonata" (Op. 27, No. 2)—"*alla damigella contessa Giulietta Guicciardi.*" It was in 1802, when he was thirty-two and she eighteen, that he wrote her so luscious name on the lintel of that sonata, so deep with yearning, so delicious in its middle mood, and so passionately despairing in its close. She had been his pupil. She told Otto Jahn long years after, when she was sixty-eight years old, that Beethoven had first inscribed to her the Rondo, Op. 51, No. 2, but, in his fickle way, he transcribed it to the Countess Lichnowsky, and put her own name over the "Moonlight Sonata" instead.

It was probably the beauty and tender reciprocation of Giulietta that inspired Beethoven to write to Wegeler in 1801:

> "Life has been a little brighter to me of late, since I have mingled more with my fellows. I think you can have no idea, how sad, how intensely desolate, my life has been during the last two years. My deafness, like a spectre, appears before me everywhere, so that I flee from society, and am obliged to act the part of a misanthrope, though you know I am not one by nature. This change has been wrought by a dear, fascinating girl, whom I love, and who loves me. After two years, I bask again in the sunshine of happiness, and now, for the first time, I feel what a truly happy state marriage might be. Unfortunately, she is not of my rank in life. Were it otherwise, I could not marry now, of course; so I must drag along valiantly. But for my deafness, I should long ago have compassed half the world with my art—I must do it still. There exists for me no greater happiness than working at and exhibiting my art. I will meet my fate boldly. It shall never succeed in crushing me."

But Giulietta went over to the great majority of Beethoven's sweethearts, and married wisely otherwise. Three years after, at her father's behest, she wedded a writer of ballet music, the Count Gallenberg, to whom Beethoven later advanced money. Twenty years afterward, in 1823, Beethoven wrote in one of those conversation-books which his deafness compelled him to use: "I was well beloved of her, more than ever her husband was loved. She came to see me and wept, but I scorned her." (He wrote it in French, "J'étais bien aimé d'elle, et plus que jamais son époux.... Et elle cherche moi pleurant, mais je la méprisais"), and he added: "If I had parted thus with my strength as well as my life, what would have remained to me for nobler and better things?"

Giulietta was long credited with being the woman to whom he wrote those three famous letters, or rather the one with the two postscripts, found in the secret drawer of an old cabinet after his death, and addressed to his "unsterbliche Geliebte." They were written in pencil, and either were copies or first draughts, or were never sent. They show his Titanic passion in full flame, and are worth quoting entire. Thayer gives them in an appendix, in the original, but I quote Lady Wallace's translation, with a few literalising changes:

"MY ANGEL, MY ALL, MY SELF—only a few words to-day, and they with a pencil (with yours!). My lodgings cannot be surely fixed until to-morrow. What a useless loss of time over such things! Why this deep grief when Necessity decides?—can our love exist without sacrifices, and by refraining from desiring all things? Can you alter the fact that you are not wholly mine, nor I wholly yours? Ah, God! contemplate the beauties of Nature, and reconcile your spirit to the inevitable. Love demands all, and rightly; so it is with me toward you and with you toward me; but you forget so easily that I must live both for you and for myself. Were we wholly united, you would feel this sorrow as little as I should.

"My journey was terrible. I did not arrive here till four o'clock yesterday morning, as no horses were to be had. The drivers chose another route; but what a dreadful one it was! At the last stage I was warned not to travel through the night, and to beware of a certain wood, but this only incited me to go forward, and I was wrong. The carriage broke down, owing to the execrable roads, mere deep rough country lanes, and had it not been for the postilions I must have been left by the wayside. Esterházy, travelling the usual road, had the same fate with eight horses as I with four. Still I felt a certain degree of pleasure, which I invariably do when I have happily surmounted any difficulty. But I must now pass from the outer to the inner man. We shall soon meet again; to-day I cannot impart to you all the reflections I have made, during the last few days, on my life; were our hearts closely united for ever, none of these would occur to me.

"My breast is overflowing with all I have to say to you. Ah! there are moments when I find that speech is nothing at all. Take courage! Continue to be ever my true and only love, my all! as I am yours. The rest the gods must ordain— what must and shall become of us.

"Your faithful

LUDWIG."

"MONDAY EVENING, *July* 6th.

"You grieve! My dearest being! I have just heard that the letters must be sent off very early. Mondays and Thursdays are the only days when the post goes to K—from here.

"You grieve! Ah! where I am, there you are also with me; how earnestly shall I strive to pass my life with you, and what a life will it be!!!! Now!!!! without you and persecuted by the kindness of people here and there, which I as little wish to deserve as they do deserve—the servility of man towards his fellow man—it pains me—and when I regard myself as a part of the universe, what am I? what is he who is called the greatest?—and yet herein is shown the godlike part of humanity! I weep in thinking that you will receive no intelligence from me till probably Saturday. However dearly you may love me, I love you more fondly still. Never disguise yourself from me. Good night! As a patient at these baths, I must now go to rest." [A few words are here effaced by Beethoven himself.] "Oh, God, so near! so far! Is not our love a truly celestial mansion, but firm as the vault of heaven itself?"

"GOOD MORNING, *July* 7th.

"Even in my bed, still my thoughts throng to you, my immortal Beloved!—now and then full of joy, and yet again sad, waiting to see whether Fate will hear us. I must live either wholly with you, or not at all. Indeed, I have resolved to wander far from you till I can fly into your arms, and feel that they are my home, and send forth my soul in unison with yours into the realm of spirits. Alas! it must be so! You will take courage, for you know my fidelity. Never can another possess my heart—never, never! Oh, God! why must one fly from what he so fondly loves? and yet my existence in W—was as miserable as here. Your love made me at once the most happy and the most unhappy of men. At my age, life requires a uniform equality; can this be found in our mutual relations? Angel! I have this moment heard that the post goes every day, so I must conclude, that you may get this letter the sooner. Be calm! for we can only attain our object of living together by the calm contemplation of our existence. Be calm—love me—to-day—yesterday— what longings with tears for you—you! you!—my life!—my all! Farewell! Oh! love me well—and never doubt the faithful heart of your beloved L.

"Ever thine.
"Ever mine.
"Ever each other's."

These impassioned letters to his "immortal beloved" were believed by Schindler to have been intended for Giulietta, and dated by him at first in 1803 and then in 1806. But Thayer, after showing how careless Beethoven was of dates, and how inaccurate, decides that these letters could not have been written before 1804. Since Giulietta was married Nov. 3, 1803, to Count Gallenberg, she could not have been the one whose life he hoped to share.

Who then remains? Thayer suggests that the woman thus honoured may have been another Thérèse, the Countess Thérèse von Brunswick. She was the cousin of Giulietta, whose husband said of Beethoven that Thérèse "adored him." About the time of these letters, he wrote to her brother, "Kiss your sister Thérèse," and later he dedicated to her his sonata, Op. 78. Some months after this he gave up his marriage scheme. Of Thérèse, Thayer says that she lived to a great age—"*ça va sans dire!*—" and was famed for a noble and large-hearted, but eccentric character. As for remembrance of Beethoven, one may apply to her the words of Shakespeare, 'She died and gave no sign.' Was it perhaps that she did not dare?

Even after seeing the above words in type, I am able to add something more definite to Thayer's argument—if one is to believe a book I stumbled on in an old bookshop, and have not found mentioned in any of the Beethoven bibliographies. The book bears every sign of telling the truth, as it makes no effort at the charms of fiction. It is by Miriam Tenger, who claims to have known the Countess Thérèse well for many years, and who describes the adoration with which her friends regarded her, the painter Peter von Cornelius calling her "the most remarkable woman I have ever known."

"She was a scholar in the classics, a piano pupil of Mozart and Beethoven," he went on, "and a woman who must have been rarely beautiful in her youth. Only a perfectly pure spirit could give the gentle look in her large, dark eyes. She spoke with inimitable beauty and clearness, because she was inwardly so transparent and beautiful, almost like a beatified spirit."

He told Fräulein Tenger the story of an early encounter of

Thérèse and Beethoven. She was a pupil who felt for him that mingled love and terror he instilled in women. One bitterly cold and stormy day he came to give the young countess her lesson; she was especially eager to please him, but grew so anxious that her playing went all askew. He was under the obsession of one of his savageries. He grew more and more impatient with her, and finally struck her hand from the keys, and rushed out bareheaded into the storm.

Her first horror at his brutality faded before her fear for his health. "Without hat! Without cloak! Good heavens!" she cried. Seizing them, she rushed after him—she, the countess, pursued the music-teacher like a valet! A servant followed her, and took the things from her hand to give to Beethoven, while she unseen returned; her mother rebuked her and ordered her to her room. But the lessons continued, and in Thérèse's diary Beethoven appeared constantly as "mon maître," "mon maître chéri."

She was doomed to a long jealousy. She saw Beethoven fall in love with her cousin Giulietta Guicciardi. Giulietta came to her for advice, saying that she longed to throw over Count Gallenberg for "that beautiful horrible Beethoven—if it were not such a come-down." She did not condescend, as we have seen, and lived to regret it bitterly.

The idolatry of the pupil finally seized the teacher. Beethoven came to dote upon the large heart, the pure soul, and the serene mind of Thérèse. One night, as he extemporised as only he could, he sang a song of love to her. One day he said, suddenly:

"I have been like a foolish boy who gathered stones and did not observe the flower growing by the way."

It was in the spring of 1806 that they became engaged. Only her brother Franz, who revered Beethoven, was in the secret. They dared not tell Thérèse's mother, but Beethoven took up life and art with a new and thorough zest. Of course, being Beethoven, he waxed wroth often at the delay and the secrecy. But the sun broke through again. For four years of his life the engagement endured. Beethoven, it seems, at last grew furious.

He quarrelled with Franz, and in 1810 one day in a frenzy snapped the bond with Thérèse. As she herself told Fräulein Tenger, "The word that parted us was not spoken by me, but by him. I was terribly frightened, turned deadly pale, and trembled." Even after this, the demon in him might have been exorcised, but Thérèse had grown afraid of the lightnings of his wrath, and fear outweighed love in the girl's heart. Sometimes she felt ashamed, in later years, of her timidity; at other times she was glad that she had not hampered his art, as any wife must have done. But now she returned him his letters. He destroyed them all, evidently, except the famous letter to his "immortal beloved," which he had written in July, 1806, soon after the betrothal; and with it he kept a portrait she had given him. As for Thérèse, she, too, had kept a copy of this letter, and as she told Fräulein Tenger:

"I have read it so often that I know it by heart—like a poem— and was it not a beautiful poem? I can only humbly say to myself, 'That man loved thee,' and thank God for it."

She also showed a sheet of old paper, with a spray of immortelles, and on it an inscription from Ludwig:

"L'immortelle à son Immortelle. Luigi."

These immortelles she sewed into a white silk cushion, with a request that it be placed under her head in her coffin.

When Fräulein Tenger had first met the countess as a child she had been asked to go every year on March 27th and lay a wreath of immortelles on Beethoven's grave. The acquaintance continued, and they met again at long intervals till the countess's death in 1861. Fraulein Tenger wrote her book in her old age when she had lost her diaries, but enough of her reminiscences remain to prove Thayer's ingenious guesses correct.

Thérèse von Brunswick was Beethoven's "Immortal Beloved," and the picture found with the letter was her portrait. It was painted by Lampi, when Thérèse was about twenty-eight; and on the frame can be seen still the words:

Countess Thérèse von Brunswick

"To the rare genius, to the great artist, to the good man, from T.B."

The picture is in the Beethoven Museum at Bonn, and in the National Museum at Pesth is a bust of Thérèse in her later years, erected in her honour because she organised out of her charity the first infants' school in the Austrian empire, and did many other good works. It is both pity and solace that the noble woman did not wed Beethoven. She was his muse for years. That was, as she said, something to thank God for. She was also a beautiful spiritual influence on him.

Once the Baron Spaun found Beethoven kissing Thérèse's portrait and muttering: "Thou wast too noble—too like an angel." The baron withdrew silently, and returning later found Beethoven extemporising in heavenly mood. He explained: "My good angel has appeared to me."

In 1813 he wrote in his diary:

> "What a fearful state to be in, not to be able to trample down all my longings for the joys of a home, to be always revelling in these longings. O God! O God! look down in mercy upon poor, unhappy Beethoven, and put an end to this soon; let it not last much longer!"

And so Beethoven never married. The women, indeed, whom he loved, whom he proposed to, always awoke with a shock to the risk of joining for life a man of such explosive whims, of such absorption in his own self and art, of such utter deafness, untidiness, and morose habit of mind.

But Beethoven himself was not always eager to wed. He could write to Gleichenstein:

> "Now you can help me get a wife. If you find a pretty one— one who may perhaps lend a sigh to my harmonies, do the courting for me. But she must be beautiful; I cannot love anything that is not beautiful; if I could, I should fall in love with myself."

One feels here a touch of disdain and frivolity. Yet he could grow fervid in such an outcry as that of his forty-sixth year:

> "Love, and love alone, can give me a happy life. O God! let me find her who will keep me in the path of virtue, the one I may rightly call my own."

Again, he could coldly rejoice that he had not sacrificed any of his individuality, or any of his devotion to music, to Giulietta Guicciardi. And the diary of Fanny Giannatasio, whose father took care of Beethoven's nephew, quotes a conversation Beethoven held on the subject of wedlock. According to this, he said that marriage should not be so indissoluble, liberty-crushing a bond; that a marriage without love was best, but that no marriages were happy. He added:

> "For himself he was excessively glad that not one of the girls had become his wife, whom he had passionately loved in former days, and thought at the time it would be the highest joy on earth to possess."

To this cynic wisdom, the poor Fanny Giannatasio del Rio, whose love for Beethoven would never have been known had not her diary enambered it for publication after her death, adds the words: "I will not repeat my answer, but I think I know a girl who, beloved by him, would not have made his life unhappy."

Ay, there's the rub! Could any one have woven a happiness about the life of that ferocious master of art, that pinioned, but struggling, victim of fate?

A CHAPTER FROM
The Love Affairs of Great Musicians, Volume 1, 1905

BEETHOVEN

By Francis Jameson Rowbotham

It was a beautiful spring morning; the sun shone in a cloudless sky, and the birds were singing blithely on the branches of the trees just outside the window, as if inviting the child who stood within to come out into the sunshine and be as free and happy as themselves. But he could not respond to their call, for he was not yet half-way through his long task. A pitiful little figure he made, mounted on a footstool in front of the pianoforte, with his head resting wearily on his hand, and his absent, dreamy gaze fixed upon the window. Scarcely five years old, and yet condemned to practise endless finger-exercises until his eyes grew dim with straining over the notes; kept a prisoner indoors, apart from his playmates, when the sun was shining and the birds were singing—and all because he happened to possess a great gift for music, and because his father, realising this fact, had determined to use the child's talents for the support of the family.

Suddenly the door of the sitting-room opened, and a stern face was thrust inside.

'Ludwig!'—the tone was harsh and severe, and at the well-known sound the boy awoke from his reverie—'Ludwig! what are you doing? Go on with your exercise at once, and remember there will be no soup for you until it is finished.'

Then the door closed again, and Ludwig turned with a sigh to his monotonous task. Why should his life be made so much harder than that of other children? he might have asked himself bitterly. It was not that he disliked music—no, he loved it—but he yearned for the brightness and sympathy which seemed to be given freely to others, and yet were denied to him. And as he strove to master his long exercise his eyes wandered from the music to a portrait which hung over the piano. It represented an elderly gentleman with a kindly face, bushy dark hair, and large dark eyes. It was a humorous face, not handsome, yet frank and pleasant, and decidedly clever. How clearly Ludwig could recall the bright blue coat, with its large gilt buttons, which the artist had faithfully portrayed! As the boy's glance rested upon the portrait the recollection of the merry times he had spent with his grandfather was presented to his mind. Once more he heard the old man's genial laugh, and felt the gentle pressure of his hand upon his curls. And then his playing! How little Ludwig had listened enrapt whilst Grandfather Ludwig charmed forth those mysterious melodies which seemed to be locked up at other times in the silent, prim little clavier! Those were delicious day-dreams that Grandfather Ludwig had the power to conjure up in his grandson's mind. But two years had passed since the kindly old musician had gone to his rest, and during those years the surroundings of Ludwig's childhood had changed for the worse.

The parents of Ludwig van Beethoven, as the boy was named, were extremely poor. Johann Beethoven, the father, was a member of the Court band of the Elector of Cologne, at Bonn, in which town Ludwig was born on December 16, 1770. The German Princes of those days maintained companies of musicians for the performance of Divine service in their chapels, as well as for their private entertainment, and such companies frequently comprised musicians of considerable ability. Johann's position as tenor singer was but a humble one, bringing in not more than £25 a year. The grandfather, who also belonged to the band, first as bass singer, and later as music director, had, on the other hand, achieved a considerable reputation, both as performer and composer, and during his latter years his earnings had gone far to support Johann's family, with whom he lived. With the old man's death, however, this help ceased, and the family means became greatly reduced.

It was, no doubt, in consequence of the privation felt at this time that the father was induced to keep Ludwig so hard at work. Mozart as a boy had exhibited marvellous powers, and his performances in public at an early age were attended by success. Johann, therefore, seemed to think that his little son would have a chance of earning money by his forced capacities for music. That a child of such tender years should have been regarded in the light of a bread-winner for the family appears unreasonable and hard; and it is not to be wondered at that Ludwig failed to understand the necessity which led to such pressure being put upon him. In his mother, Marie Magdalena, however, he could always find a ready sympathy and a tenderness which must have served to counteract, to some degree, the unhappiness occasioned by the father's severity. But not even a mother's love could make up for the loss the child had sustained by his grandfather's death, for the excellent qualities of head and heart which the old man had exhibited were just those which the boy missed in his father. To Ludwig music meant everything— or, rather, it would have meant everything, even at that early time, had its development only been continued under the same kindly influence.

Despite his severity and unreasonableness, however, Johann must be credited with the determination that his boy's knowledge of music should be as thorough as it was possible to make it with the means at his command, and to this end he spared no pains. Moreover, in order that Ludwig should not grow up in complete ignorance of subjects which lay outside his art, he was sent to the public school of Bonn to pick up what learning he could, though this chiefly comprised reading and writing. With his schoolfellows Ludwig had little in common. They thought him shy, because he kept to himself, and showed no desire to join in their games. The truth was his mind was almost wholly absorbed by music, and the consciousness that this great love had taken possession of his soul, and was growing stronger day by day may have made him inapt for games or boyish society, and thus may have led to his taking refuge in his own thoughts. In the companionship of music he could never have felt lonely, and in his walks between school hours he found plenty to interest him. He never tired of sounding Nature for her harmonies, and as he pursued his way through the fields and lanes he listened to the peasants singing at their work, and then, catching up the simple tunes, he fitted his own notes to them, so as to produce beautiful and subtle effects of harmony. Many of those old folk-tunes were closely connected with the history of the country to which they belonged; they were often the musical expression of the feelings, struggles, and passions of the people, and to Beethoven's sensitive ear they conveyed a deeper meaning than they did to the simple peasants who hummed or carolled them to the whirr of the spinning-wheel, the blows of the forge-hammer, or the speeding of the plough.

Thus, with the drudgery of unremitting toil and constant reproof, the years passed away until Ludwig was nearly nine. Hard as the lessons of those years had been, there could be no doubt as to the progress which he had made. Not even the severity and harshness of his father could lessen or abate his yearning for musical knowledge; and so it came about that one day Johann, regarding him with an expression more akin to pride and satisfaction than that which Ludwig was accustomed to read in his father's face, said, 'I can teach you no more; we must see about finding you another master.'

But how this was to be accomplished it is as difficult for us as it must have been to Johann himself to imagine; for, so far from the family circumstances having improved, the poverty was even more acute than before, and such further efforts as the father may have been induced to make to increase their comforts were negatived by his growing addiction to drink—a fact which must of itself have caused a further reduction in their resources. Fortunately, at this critical period help was forthcoming in the shape of a musician boarder, who agreed to give instruction to Ludwig in part return for his accommodation.

The coming of Tobias Pfeiffer, as the new boarder was named, must have been regarded by Ludwig with some curiosity. Would he turn out an even harder task-master than his own father had been? This question was soon settled by the glimpse which Tobias early gave to his pupil of his peculiar method of imparting instruction. Johann's evenings were now chiefly spent at some tavern resort, whither it became the custom for Tobias to repair at a very late hour, in order that he might give his drunken landlord a safe convoy home. By this friendly help the erring Johann escaped falling into the hands of the police—an eventuality which would have resulted in his losing his employment. Having fulfilled his friendly mission, Pfeiffer would betake himself to Ludwig's bedside, and, with a shake which soon became familiar, would arouse the boy with, 'Now then, Ludwig, time for practice!' At this gentle admonition the sleepy child would rise obediently, rubbing his eyes, and master and pupil descended to the sitting-room, where they would play together till the early hours of the morning—Pfeiffer giving out a theme, and Beethoven extemporising upon it, and then Ludwig in his turn giving the lead to Pfeiffer. Extemporisation would be followed by duets, until the approach of day gave warning that it was time to retire to bed. Such music as these two players made in the still hours of the night was, no doubt, but rarely heard in the district in which they lived, and on the other side of the open window, in the early dawn of the summer morning, a small knot of listeners frequently gathered, attracted by the unusual performance proceeding within.

For about a year this curious mode of instruction continued, and during this time Ludwig's education received a stimulus in the shape of lessons in Latin, French, Italian, and Logic, given by a man named Zambona. This Zambona was an eccentric personage, whose peculiarities would appear to have been well adapted to the condition of things prevailing in the Beethoven home.

He apparently considered himself qualified to fill a variety of posts, as he had acted as innkeeper, chamber-porter at the Court, and book-keeper, in addition to being a teacher of languages; but his worth was proved by the fact that Beethoven made good progress under his tuition. Hitherto Ludwig's playing had been confined to the pianoforte and violin, but at this point a friendly hand was held out to him by an old friend of his grandfather, named Van den Eeden, who for many years had held the post of organist at the Court. 'Come to me, and I will teach you the organ,' the kindly old musician said to Ludwig, and the boy's heart leapt with pleasure at the generous offer. No doubt Van den Eeden saw in the young player the signs of genius such as his old friend had exhibited in no small degree in past years, and felt drawn towards him in consequence. A new field was thus opened to Beethoven, and when, at the end of a year, Van den Eeden resigned on account of ill-health, and the post was given to Christian Neefe, Ludwig was happy in the discovery of a new friend, who not only expressed his willingness to carry on the instruction, but was quick to recognise the boy's extraordinary talent. At this point of our story we get our first glimpse of the fruits of Beethoven's work at composition. The death of a friend who had assisted the family with money gifts inspired him to write a cantata in his honour; but though it was performed at the funeral, no trace exists for us of this little outcome of gratitude on Beethoven's part.

Ludwig was now ten years old, and in the winter of 1781 he made his first essay at bread-winning for the family. The state of things at home was wretched in the extreme, and the hopelessness of looking to the father to retrieve the condition into which they had fallen decided Ludwig's mother upon undertaking a tour through Holland with the boy, in the hope that his playing at the houses of the rich might bring in money. We may well believe that sheer necessity alone impelled the gentle, ailing woman to such a step. Her faith in her son's powers was evidently of a higher order than that of Johann, and she must have seen that this exhibition of his talents at so early an age not only implied an interruption to his studies, but also, to some extent, a debasing of the art which she felt that he loved for its own sake. The tour produced money—that chiefest need of the moment—and, so far, it was a success; but Ludwig himself did not carry away any pleasing recollections of his visit. 'The Dutch are very stingy, and I shall take care not to trouble them again,' he afterwards remarked to a friend; and there was no repetition of the experiment.

In the following year a notice appeared in *Cramer's Magazine*, calling the attention of music-lovers to a young player who, though not more than eleven years old, could play with force and finish, read well at sight, and—most remarkable of all—play the greater part of Bach's 'Wohltemperirte Klavier' (Well-tempered Clavier), 'a feat,' declared the writer, 'which will be understood by the initiated.' 'This young genius,' the article went on to say, 'deserves some assistance that he may travel. If he goes on as he has begun, he will certainly become a second Mozart.'

The writer of this notice was Christian Neefe, and the subject of his praise was none other than his pupil, Ludwig Beethoven. That the boy should have mastered a work of such extraordinary difficulty as Bach's collection of preludes and fugues may well have excited the astonishment of his friend and teacher, whose praise was thus deservedly given. But Neefe's confidence in his pupil's abilities was shown in a more substantial manner during this same year. Van den Eeden's death took place in June, and when the Court band had played the old organist to his last resting-place Neefe received orders to proceed with the rest of the performers to Münster, whither the Elector had already gone. Two days before the band left Bonn Neefe called Beethoven to his side, and told him that he was going away for a time. 'I must have a deputy to take my place at the organ here,' continued the organist, looking keenly into his pupil's face as he spoke. 'Now, tell me, who do you think I ought to appoint to the post?'

Ludwig's face was crossed by a shade of trouble. If his kind tutor was going away, how did he know whether he would find his deputy equally willing to teach him? But Christian Neefe was waiting for his answer, and his eyes were shining with a kindly, half-amused light. 'I do not know,' Ludwig began hesitatingly. But Neefe's eyes had grown serious, and he now spoke with earnestness.

'I have thought of a deputy, Ludwig, and I think I can trust him—yes, I am sure I may trust him. The deputy shall be yourself!'

Beethoven's surprise and delight may be imagined. But Neefe knew what he was about, and in this preferment we may mark the first step in the recognition of Beethoven's genius. The honour was great. To be entrusted with the conduct of Divine service at the chapel, and to receive the deference due to the position of organist—it must have seemed incredible to Ludwig at first; and he was only eleven and a half! To his mother he must first have carried the good news, and if the father's expression had in it less of joy and thankfulness than hers it must be attributed to the fact that no pay was attached to the exalted position which Ludwig had obtained.

Beethoven had now practically the choice of three instruments to select from; but his heart did not waver for long, ere it became fixed upon the pianoforte as the fittest interpreter of his genius, and he was true to his first love to the end. His 'Three Sonatas for the Pianoforte,' written about this time, gives us the first record of his published works. Evidently those terrible finger exercises were beginning to bear fruit, for the young musician had acquired considerable command over the instrument of his choice—indeed, his musical life was now beginning to open itself before him, and the longing to do great things had taken possession of his soul. There were no more tears at being forced to work, for the greatest incentives to work—love and ambition— were now swaying him and impelling him onwards at a speed which nothing could check. Neefe's confidence and praise were more than justified, and before he had completed his thirteenth year Beethoven received his first official appointment at the hands of the Elector. He could now sign himself 'Ludwig van Beethoven, Cembalist im Orchester,' and his duties comprised not only the playing of the pianoforte in the orchestra, but the conducting of the band at rehearsals. With this accession, however, there was still the fact staring him in the face of no money coming in. Just at this time, too, the Elector Max Friedrich died; and it was not until a year later, when Beethoven was appointed second organist to the Court, under the new Elector Max Franz, that he began to receive a small salary in return for his services. Thirteen pounds a year sounds very little for so much work and responsibility, but Ludwig was overjoyed to think that he could back up his announcement to his parents with so substantial a fact as the receipt of an income. For the poverty at home was keener than ever; Johann's earnings did not exceed £25 a year, and as his voice was steadily declining, the outlook for the family had become exceedingly black.

The time would not appear to have been propitious for joking; nevertheless, Beethoven sat in the organ-loft one day planning a joke. He had just had a conversation with one of the chief singers of the band—a tenor named Heller—and the latter had been boasting that his knowledge of singing was so great that he could easily surmount any difficulty as it presented itself. Beethoven inherited from his grandfather a love of joking, and the temptation to lower the singer's vanity was too great to be resisted. Accordingly, on the following Sunday, whilst Heller was singing a solo to Ludwig's accompaniment, the latter adroitly introduced a modulation of his own. Heller unsuspectingly followed his lead, and fell into the trap devised for him, with the result that, after attempting to keep up with the organist, he lost himself entirely and, to the astonishment of the congregation, came to a dead stop; and it was only when Beethoven returned to the original key that the disconcerted singer could proceed. Heller was naturally furious at the trick played upon him, and lodged a complaint with the Elector. The latter, however, was too good a musician himself to be angry at this exhibition of skill on the part of his youngest performer, and he contented himself with admonishing Beethoven not to attempt any more clever tricks.

There was a dream which had taken possession of young Beethoven's mind at this time. It was constantly recurring during the hours of work, and when he lay down to sleep in his poorly-furnished attic it was with the hope that the dawning of a new day might bring him nearer to its realisation. Yet for some time the dream remained only a shadowy companion to his working thoughts, ever present, it is true, and sometimes glowing in brighter colours that seemed to give to it the semblance of reality—but still, only a dream. But the vision seen afar off was to be realised at length—Beethoven was to visit Vienna! It was the city of his dreams, the centre of his longings, this Vienna, just as it was the centre of the musical world of Germany at that time. A kind friend had come forward with the offer to pay his expenses for the journey, and Ludwig knew that his dream had come true.

As we have seen, the dire straits into which the family had fallen had not hindered Beethoven's pursuit of musical knowledge. His genius had steadily asserted itself under the most adverse conditions; and now we are to picture the young musician, at the age of seventeen, full of fire and energy, setting out on a journey which must have been fraught with the brightest anticipations. He was to meet in Vienna the greatest composer of the day. Mozart—the divine Mozart—was staying in the city, planning the production of his opera, 'Don Giovanni,' and it had been arranged that he should receive Beethoven and put his powers to the test.

On reaching Vienna, Ludwig made his way to Mozart's house, and with a heart beating high with expectancy, and a face aglow with excitement, he was ushered into the presence of the maestro. Mozart received him kindly, but it was evident that his thoughts were preoccupied, for, after desiring Beethoven to play, he began to turn over his papers in a listless fashion. 'Ah!' thought

Beethoven; 'he imagines that I have merely come to play him something which I have practised for the occasion.' Dismayed by this reflection, he took his hands from the keyboard and, turning to Mozart, said, 'Will you give me a theme on which to extemporise?' Aroused by his appeal, and the earnest look which accompanied it, Mozart sat down and played a simple theme; and then Beethoven, taking up the slender thread, improvised so finely—allowing his feelings to flow into the music as he went on—that a bystander could not fail to have been struck by the change which came over Mozart's face as he listened. The abstracted look gave place to one of pure astonishment. Then he arose from his seat, and, stepping softly into an adjoining room, where a number of his friends were waiting to see him, he exclaimed, 'Pay attention to this young man, for he will make a noise in the world some day.' Beethoven, meanwhile, played on and on, lost in the intricate melodies which he was weaving out of the single thread, until the touch of Mozart's hand upon his shoulder recalled him to earth to hear the master's praises sounding in his ear.

Vanished in a moment were the memories of the trials and hardships which he had undergone in order to perfect himself for this day of trial, for Beethoven realised that he possessed the power of impressing so great a judge as Mozart; and praise and encouragement were needed at that time, when he was trying to do his best, rather than later on, when his powers were assured. Nor was this the only recognition which his talents received on his visit. The fame of the young player had reached the ears of royalty itself, and he was granted an audience of the Emperor Joseph, whose love of music had made him desirous of hearing for himself what the Bonn performer could do.

Beethoven's happiness, however, was soon to be clouded by sorrow, for shortly after his return to Bonn his mother died—the mother to whom he owed so much gentleness and sympathy in his childhood; she who was always ready to forgive his outbursts of temper and impatience, and to cheer and encourage him to further effort. How deeply he felt her loss may be gathered from the letter which he wrote to a friend at the time. 'She was, indeed, a kind, loving mother to me, and my best friend. Ah! who was happier than I, when I could still utter the sweet name of mother, and it was heard? But to whom can I now say it? Only to the silent form resembling her, evoked by the power of imagination.' That her death inspired some of his most beautiful compositions we may suppose, for it is natural that his grief should have found its best expression in music. A few months later his little sister Margaretha died, and the sense of loneliness deepened.

And then something bright came into his life. He made the acquaintance of a family named Breuning, comprising a widow lady and her four children—three boys and a girl—all of about his own age. The youngest boy and the daughter became his pupils, and a close friendship sprang up between them. He stayed at the house for several days at a time, joined in their excursions, and in every way was treated as one of the family. As the Breunings were intellectual people, their friendship was a great help to Beethoven; his whole nature expanded in the sunshine of their society, and very soon he found himself taking a deep interest in the literature of his country—a subject of which he had previously been ignorant. An affection for English authors likewise grew from this intimacy with a family of wide tastes and acquirements—indeed, new interests and fresh paths of pleasant intercourse were opening to him every day, whilst the separation from the miserable surroundings of his own home invigorated him for work. Every hour that could be spared from his official duties or his teaching was devoted to study and composition. Most of his composing was done in the open air; and for this purpose he provided himself with rough sketch-books, one of which he always carried with him, so that he might jot down in it such musical ideas as occurred to him during his rambles through the lanes and fields.

It was during this happy intercourse with the Breuning family that Beethoven made the acquaintance of a generous young nobleman, with whom he not only became on the most friendly terms, but who both helped him and encouraged his talents. Count von Waldstein, as the nobleman was named, called one day on Beethoven in his poor room, and found the composer, whose works he so much admired, seated before an old, worn-out piano, on which he was elaborating one of his compositions. The Count said nothing at the time, but shortly afterwards Beethoven was astonished and delighted at receiving a fine new instrument, accompanied by a message from his friend praying his acceptance of the gift. It went to the Count's heart to observe the poverty-stricken conditions under which the composer worked. That he himself should be surrounded by every luxury, whilst the gifted musician who laboured for his enjoyment was driven to practise all manner of shifts to maintain himself in food and clothing, seemed intolerably unjust. Yet Waldstein knew and respected Beethoven too well to offend his pride by offering presents of money where no service was required in return; and so he hit upon the harmless device of helping his poor friend under the pretence that the Elector was making him an allowance. But though he opened his purse in another's name, he took care to let Beethoven see into his own heart, in order that he might there read the sympathy and affection for which, happily, no cloak was needed.

How deeply Beethoven was moved by this friendship we may understand when we listen to the grand sonata which, though it was not composed until some years later, he dedicated to the Count. We want no better title for this exquisitely beautiful work than that by which it is known to the world—the 'Waldstein Sonata.' As the grand chords which follow the opening bars strike the ear it seems as if Beethoven were speaking to his friend—speaking to him out of the fullness of his heart, out of his poverty and mean surroundings—and rising by the strengthening influence of love to a height of eloquence and grandeur which no spoken words could have attained.

The conditions at home, meanwhile, were growing worse.

Carl and Johann, Beethoven's two younger brothers, of whom no previous mention has been made, were engaged, the one in studying music, and the other as apprentice to the Court apothecary, but neither was bringing grist to the mill. The father had sunk still deeper under the degrading influence of drink, and his voice was almost ruined by his excesses, so that it had become increasingly difficult to maintain for the family even the appearance of respectability. On more than one occasion Beethoven, in returning home at night, had encountered his drunken father in the hands of the police, from whose custody he had succeeded in rescuing him only after much persuasion, and it seemed as if his discharge from the band must be merely a question of time. The state of affairs, in fact, could no longer be concealed from the Elector, who, knowing the circumstances with which Beethoven had to contend, finally ordered that a portion of the father's salary should be paid over to Ludwig, in order that the money might be properly expended for the support of the family.

Meanwhile, at the Court itself great changes had been effected in regard to the band. With a view to encouraging the growth of operatic art, the Elector had established a national theatre, and Beethoven was appointed viola player in the orchestra, in addition to retaining the post of second organist to the chapel. The numerous performances of operatic works by the company must have given Beethoven an insight into what was to him a new branch of his art, from which he did not fail to profit later on. His work in the band was not increased by the changes which had been made, and as the Elector was frequently absent from Bonn, he found ample leisure to pursue his studies in composition, and to enjoy the intellectual society of his friends. Four years thus slipped away, until the month of July, 1792, saw the Bonn musicians preparing to receive a distinguished visitor. Haydn was to pass through Bonn on his way to Vienna from London, where his compositions and playing had created a sensation, and the band had arranged a grand reception in his honour. Beethoven, of course, was amongst the invited guests on the occasion, and he seized the opportunity of submitting to the master a cantata which he had lately composed. Haydn praised the composition highly, and warmly encouraged Beethoven to go on with his studies—words which sent the young composer back to his work with glowing cheeks and a determination to accomplish greater things.

The commendation of so renowned a master as Haydn must have gone far towards convincing the Elector that by keeping Beethoven at Bonn he was burying talent and cramping powers that only required a wider scope in order to produce great works, and that, therefore, some step should now be taken to develop his genius. It was with a heart overflowing with joy and gratitude that Ludwig learnt that the kindly Max Franz had decided to send him to Vienna, at his own expense, to take lessons in strict counterpoint from Haydn. Surely this could mean nothing less than that the days of adversity and struggling with poverty had closed behind him for ever, and that a future bright with hope had opened, upon which, though he might not forecast its results, he could enter with courage and determination. He was now twenty-two, and his compositions—published and in manuscript—had brought him such fame and appreciation as the small German town could give to one born and reared within its narrow sphere. Now, however, the bonds which hitherto had fettered his genius were to be broken, and, freed from the restraint of Court duties, he would be able to give full vent to the powers which he was burning to express.

In November of this year he bade farewell to Bonn and his friends, and set forth on his journey, though not, we may be sure, without regrets at parting with such true helpers and sympathisers as Count Waldstein, the Breunings, and the man to whom he owed so much—Christian Neefe. With the last named he left these words of thanks: 'Thank you for the counsel you have so often given me on my progress in my divine art. Should I ever become a great man you will certainly have assisted in it.' In an album provided for the purpose his musical brethren inscribed their farewells, and Waldstein's message ran as follows:

'DEAR BEETHOVEN,

'You are travelling to Vienna in fulfilment of your long-cherished wish. The genius of Mozart is still weeping and bewailing the death of her favourite.[1] With the inexhaustible Haydn she found a refuge, but no occupation, and is now waiting to leave him and join herself to some one else. Labour assiduously, and receive Mozart's spirit from the hands of Haydn.

'Your old friend,

'WALDSTEIN.
'Bonn,
'*October 29, 1792.*

Little did either Beethoven or his friends imagine that he would never set foot in Bonn again, but so it was to be. Two years later war had broken out with France, Bonn was captured by the French Republican army, and the Elector and his retinue were forced to fly the town. Those two years had witnessed great strides in the march of Beethoven's career. He had arrived in Vienna as a comparatively unknown musician—though not, it is true, without recommendations from Count Waldstein—but his marvellous command of the pianoforte, and, more especially, his powers of extemporisation, had electrified his hearers to such a degree as to secure for him a place in the front rank of performers of the day. He was a constant visitor at the houses of the aristocracy, with several members of whom he had become on terms of intimacy. In the Prince and Princess Karl Lichnowsky he had found true friends and sincere admirers, who not only welcomed him as one of the family, but provided apartments for him in their house, and bestowed upon him an annuity of £60. Many who had heard him play forthwith engaged him as teacher, and on every hand his genius and powers were the theme of the hour.

It is hardly to be wondered at that with all this praise and patronage on the part of the wealthy aristocracy (and it is necessary to bear in mind that in Vienna at that time the musical profession was entirely dependent upon the patronage of the nobility), Beethoven should have encountered considerable hostility from other members of his profession. For a good deal of the enmity which his success aroused he himself was no doubt to blame; he took no pains to please or conciliate, and he showed even more independence towards the rich and great than towards those of his own rank. The result was that only those who could afford to overlook his faults for the sake of his genius—and for the sake of something else which lay beneath his crust of obstinate pride and openly expressed disregard for rank and wealth—remained constant to him. Of his obstinacy and self-will several instances will be given in the course of our story; but it is necessary at this point to draw attention to the early period at which this determined force of character began to assert itself. It is an astonishing fact, and one that demonstrates the extraordinary power of Beethoven's genius, that in spite of everything that could be urged against him—his origin, rudeness of manner and speech, refusal to pay homage to the great—even his youth and the comparative shortness of the time during which he had been before the public—Beethoven should have not only won a front place as a performer, but also retained the sincere regard and respect of men and women belonging to the worthiest as well as the highest ranks of society.

In the midst of the whirl of work and entertainment into which the musical life of Vienna had plunged him, Beethoven was constant to those whom he had left behind him at Bonn. He had not been absent more than a month before he received news of his father's death. There had been very little affection in his heart for the parent whose severity had called forth his childish tears, and whose selfish indulgence had increased the burden of his mother's existence, nor was Beethoven the man to pretend what he did not feel. But with the father's death the allowance which had been paid through Ludwig for the support of the two sons, Carl and Johann, ceased, and this fact awoke Beethoven to instant action. He wrote to the Elector begging that the grant might be continued for his sake, and the request was granted. Later on we shall see to what extent he carried his affection for at least one of these brothers.

With the Prince and Princess Lichnowsky Beethoven shortly became, as we have said, on terms of the greatest intimacy. All Vienna looked to the house of Lichnowsky for patronage and help wherever art or science was concerned, and none looked in vain. To Beethoven—young, rough, and almost untutored in the usages of society, but with his commanding genius and his equally remarkable personality—the Lichnowskys were kindness itself. The Princess saw to his comforts, and arranged his engagements in the same motherly fashion as Madame Breuning had done after his mother's death, whilst the Prince even went so far in his consideration for Beethoven's sensitiveness as to direct his servants to attend to the musician's bell before answering his own. Extreme sensibility to what he deemed indifference or neglect on the part of his friends was undoubtedly one of Ludwig's chief weaknesses; but he resented angrily the Prince's discovery of the fact, and to mark his displeasure he immediately engaged a servant of his own to wait upon him. The regularity of the household arrangements at the palace was another matter which grated against Beethoven's love of Bohemianism; to be forced to dress for dinner, especially at a set hour of the day, was to him an abomination not to be suffered. The workings of his genius were not to be regulated by the clockwork contrivances of civilised life, and hence he first took to dining out at some tavern, where he could be at his ease, and finally went altogether into lodgings. But the Prince and Princess, like the good, sensible people they were, only smiled at the vagaries of their favourite, and if his seat at their table was henceforth but too frequently vacant, they kept for him a warm corner in their hearts; whilst, as for Beethoven himself, his affection for his kind friends remained as strong as ever.

Careless as he was with regard both to dress and manners, there was no trace of either carelessness or haste in his compositions, and he was most insistent in having the latter performed in exact accordance with his plans. One night, when his great work 'Leonore' was to be rehearsed, the third bassoon failed to put in an appearance, and Beethoven stamped about in a fury, heaping execrations upon the head of the absent player. Prince Lobkowitz, who was present, and who was one of Beethoven's chief patrons, laughed heartily at the composer's outburst, and then tried to calm him by saying: 'Well, well, what does it matter? You have the first and second bassoons safely here, surely the third man doesn't count for much.' The rehearsal was at length allowed to proceed, but Beethoven could not forget that his judgment had been questioned by the Prince's mocking laughter, and as soon as the performance had ended and the company had dispersed, he rushed across the Platz to the gates of the Lobkowitz Palace, and shouted at the top of his voice: 'Lobkowitzscher Esel! Lobkowitzscher Esel!' ('Ass of a Lobkowitz! Ass of a Lobkowitz!')

Beethoven's temper was of the passionate order that is apt to explode at the slightest provocation, and when once aroused he seemed to lose all power of self-control. As one of his greatest friends[2] has remarked, he needed at his elbow some one who possessed the ability to give a humorous turn to what was spoken in the heat of the moment, so as to put them all on good terms with one another again. As it was, he would say the unkindest things even to his greatest friends, and afterwards bitterly regret having said them. His manners were rude and abrupt, but his great genius, combined with the absolute simplicity and straightforwardness of his character, won him his way everywhere.

A personality so rare as Beethoven's had a charm for those who worshipped genius, and thus he was forgiven speeches which no one else in his position would have dared to utter. He manifested complete indifference with regard to what people said of him or of his works—only when his honour was in any way impeached did he blaze forth in his own defence. He hated deception of any kind; in both heart and action he was as open as the day, and he was quick to resent a suspicion of deception on the part of others. On one occasion a hitch occurred with regard to a performance of his works, and he suddenly suspected three of his friends of having created the obstacle for their own ends, although they had in reality been working hard to overcome the difficulty.

He accordingly sat down and wrote to each as follows:

'To COUNT LICHNOWSKY.

'Falsehoods I despise. Visit me no more. There will be no concert.

'BEETHOVEN.'

* * * * *

'To HERR SCHINDLER.

'Visit me no more until I send for you. No concert.

'BEETHOVEN.'

* * * * *

'To Herr Schuppanzigh.

'Visit me no more. I give no concert.

'Beethoven.'

Haydn and Beethoven did not get on well together; there seems to have been something antagonistic in their natures which prevented anything approaching to reciprocal feeling between them. Beethoven from the first considered that he had a grievance against his master in the fact that he did not make sufficient progress, owing to Haydn's being so much occupied with his own work. This dissatisfaction led to his seeking guidance in other quarters; but for about a year after his arrival in Vienna he refrained from doing this openly, until Haydn's departure for England gave him the opportunity of changing masters. Thereafter he took lessons every day of the week from several of the best musicians in the city both in playing and composition. Albrechtsberger was the famous contrapuntist of his day, and Beethoven derived much from his teaching; he does not appear to have impressed his master, however, with a high opinion of his powers, for the old man advised one of his pupils to have nothing to do with the young man from Bonn. 'He has learnt nothing,' Albrechtsberger added, 'and will never do anything in decent style.' This was in allusion to Beethoven's wilfulness in persistently transgressing certain established rules of composition. The old teacher failed to see that Beethoven's refusal to be bound by hard-and-fast rules arose, not from mere caprice, but from the force of a genius which would not submit to be trammelled by any kind of artificial limitations. The wisdom of Beethoven is, however, shown by the fact that he wrote out his exercises with the most scrupulous care, and in exact accordance with what were regarded as the laws of composition, for his genius, great and original as it was, would not presume upon ignorance.

But who could resist the young player when he seated himself at the pianoforte and began one of those wonderful improvisations about which so much has been written, but of the effect of which we can only faintly judge by the fact that the hearers were held spellbound until the finish? Who amongst that audience, gathered from the best and most critical followers and lovers of the art that Vienna contained, gave a thought to how many rules had been broken, or were likely to be broken, by the player, or, indeed, had room for any other thought but one of admiration for the music which was filling their ears and charming their senses? 'His improvisation was most brilliant and striking,' wrote Karl Czerny, the player and composer, and pupil of Beethoven; 'in whatever company he might chance to be he knew how to produce such an effect upon every hearer that frequently not an eye remained dry, while many would break out into loud sobs; for there was something wonderful in his expression, in addition to the beauty and originality of his ideas, and his spirited style of rendering them.' Ferdinand Ries, another of his pupils, has declared that no other artist that he ever heard could approach Beethoven in extemporisation. 'The wealth of ideas which forced themselves on him, the caprices to which he surrendered himself, the variety of treatment, the difficulties, were inexhaustible,' And it must be borne in mind that in respect to this art Beethoven was brought into competition with several older and undoubtedly brilliant performers of the day, who, until he came amongst them, had swayed their respective circles of admirers.

Yet, strangely enough, the emotion aroused in his hearers seemed to find no response in Beethoven himself. Frequently when he discovered how deeply he had moved his audience he would burst into roars of laughter; at other times the sight of their emotion stirred him up to angry resentment, and he would shout, 'We artists don't want tears, we want applause!' That a player should open his soul in his music and then abuse his audience for their inability to suppress the feelings which he had aroused appears strange indeed. But the caprice and wilfulness which marked his public playing are shown equally in his relations with people in everyday life. What may have been his true feelings is concealed—it is only the mask which is seen; and the mask was so constantly worn that it no doubt deceived many. Every now and again, however, we get a glimpse of his true nature in his intercourse with those who knew him best. Irritable to a degree, and occasionally outrageous as his conduct appears to have been, it needed but the touch of another's grief to draw from him the golden thread of sympathy. On one occasion he offended the susceptibilities of the company assembled in one of the most fashionable drawing-rooms of Vienna by using his hostess's snuffers as a toothpick! Yet, later on, when that household was plunged into mourning by the loss of a beloved child, and visitors were denied, it was Beethoven to whom the bereaved mother opened her doors, and to whom she turned for sympathy.

It is much to be regretted that the nobility of nature which was really and truly Beethoven's attribute should have been so constantly overshadowed and dominated by something else which, without being a superior force, seemed by a strange perversity to be always to the fore. Whilst, however, we would wish to give to every instance of his goodness of heart its fullest weight, it would be useless, as well as wrong, to endeavour to hide the fact that his conduct, even towards those who desired to be his friends, and to whom he owed obligations for acts of sympathy and kindness, frequently admitted of no excuse. His anger, though sharp, was short, and left no sting behind; but his unjust suspicions and scornful treatment of men whose confidence he had won by his genius and force of character, were the cause of sorrow and suffering to those whom he attacked, as well as of remorse to himself, whereby his whole life was embittered, and his better nature warped to ignoble ends.

The good people of Vienna must, indeed, have been somewhat at a loss how to take the genius who had thus burst into their midst and laid them under captivity. Attempts at conciliation were more often than not frustrated by his variable temperament; for though none was apter than Beethoven to take offence, there was no one quicker to resent any effort at mediation by a third party, on whose unfortunate head it was only too likely that the irate composer would empty the vials of his wrath. Nevertheless, his erratic behaviour did not sensibly lessen the circle of his admirers or diminish the popularity which his fame had brought him. Many of the fashionable ladies of Vienna came to him for lessons instead of requiring his attendance at their houses; but such condescension made no difference to the man who held that mind and character alone were the qualifications by which men and women were to be weighed in the social balance. If, therefore, the young ladies talked or showed inattention during their lessons, he became furious, and would tear up the music and scatter it over the floor. His rage, indeed, seems to have been quite ungovernable at times. On one occasion he was playing a duet with his pupil Ries when his ear caught some fragments of a conversation which a young nobleman was carrying on with a lady at the further end of the room. Instantly he jumped up from the piano in a rage, and, taking Ries's hands off the keyboard, he bellowed, 'I play no longer for such hogs!' nor could either apologies or entreaties induce him to resume the performance.

It was often a matter of some difficulty to get him to play, especially when he was not in the humour. On such occasions he would preface the performance by striking the keys with the palm of his hand, or draw his finger along the keyboard from end to end, roaring with laughter, and in other ways behave like a spoiled child. He would not bear being pressed beyond a certain point. Once, it is related, he was asked to play before strangers at the country-house of one of his rich patrons, and flatly refused to comply; whereupon the host jokingly threatened that, if he would not play, he should be confined as a prisoner in the house. Beethoven on this jumped up and ran out of the mansion, and though it was night, he walked three miles to the next town, and thence posted to Vienna. The next day a bust of this patron which stood on Beethoven's bookcase fell to the ground, and was shattered to pieces![3]

His views as to the superiority of mind and character over everything else were certainly borne out by his actions. One day, when he was walking with the poet Goethe near Uplitz, the Imperial family were observed to be approaching. Goethe at once stood aside and removed his hat, at the same time plucking his friend by the sleeve, to remind him that they were in the presence of royalty. Beethoven, however, seemed to regard this as a fitting opportunity for illustrating his views on the independence of art, for, shaking off the hand that detained him, he buttoned up his coat in a determined manner, planted his hat firmly on his head, and, folding his arms behind him, marched straight into the ranks of the Imperial party! If Goethe felt dismayed at his friend's lack of respect, he must have been astonished to note the result; for the Archduke Rodolph not only made way for Beethoven to pass, but removed his hat, whilst the Empress was the first to bow to him.

In appearance Beethoven was short, broad, and strong-looking. His face was not prepossessing. 'He was meanly dressed, and very ugly to look at,' wrote a lady who knew and admired him, 'but full of nobility and fine feeling, and highly cultivated.' It must have been difficult to describe a face which was subject to such frequent changes of expression, but its forcefulness must have been apparent to every beholder. The eyes were black and bright, and they had a way of dilating when the composer was buried in thought so as to impart to his face an expression of being inspired. Gloomily abstracted as he would be at times, when possessed by some absorbing train of ideas, nothing could have been more cordial or more winning than the smile which lighted up his face at the sight of a friend. With a mass of dark hair surmounting a high and broad forehead, and the quick, penetrative glance which shot from beneath the large overhanging eyebrows, Beethoven's face must have struck the observer with a sense of its strong individuality. Nevertheless, only a few of the portraits have succeeded in conveying a true likeness of the man who was so unlike every one else. His hands were hairy, and the fingers 'strong and short, and pressed out with long practising.' He was very particular about the position of his hands when playing, and as a rule he kept his body quite still. When conducting, however, his movements were constant and curious. At a *pianissimo* passage 'he would crouch down so as to be hidden by the desk, and then, as the *crescendo* increased, would gradually rise, beating all the time, until at the *fortissimo* he would spring into the air with his arms extended, as if wishing to float on the clouds.'[4]

It was one of the most striking of Beethoven's characteristics that he dearly loved a joke. Ever since the time when he played off the rather unkind joke on the singer Heller the passion for joking had grown upon him to such an extent that evidence of its ruling force appears in every chapter of his life. He occasionally introduced a joke into his compositions. Thus, in the 'Pastoral Symphony,' we come across a trio between a nightingale, a quail, and a cuckoo. Again, in other works, such as the No. 8 Symphony, the bassoons are brought in unexpectedly, in such a manner as to produce a humorous effect. He never missed an opportunity of playing off a joke upon any of his friends, both in season and out of season, and he always showed his appreciation of the victim's discomfiture by roars of laughter. His letters are full of puns, and he bestows uncomplimentary nicknames upon his intimates. One day his brother Johann, who had acquired a small property in the neighbourhood of Vienna, called upon him in his absence, and left his card, bearing the inscription, 'Johann van Beethoven, Gutsbesitzer' (Land proprietor). Beethoven was so tickled with the conceit of this designation that he could not resist returning the card to his brother with the following inscription scrawled upon the back: 'L. van Beethoven, Hirnbesitzer' (Brain proprietor). Some of his jokes, however, were in extremely bad taste. On one occasion a lady admirer preferred a request for a lock of his hair as a keepsake, and he sent her instead a wisp cut from the beard of a goat! With his inordinate love of joking, however, he was a poor hand at bearing a joke that told against himself. It is related that, having once been rude enough to interrupt a player named Himmel in the midst of the latter's improvisation by asking when he was going to begin, Himmel afterwards wrote to him that 'the latest invention in Berlin was a lantern for the blind'—a joke which Beethoven not only failed to see, but 'when it was pointed out to him he was furious, and would have nothing more to do with his correspondent.'

His carelessness in matters of dress was very noticeable. Czerny, his pupil, has described how he found him at home on his first visit, with his shock of black hair and his unshaven chin, and his ears stuffed with cotton-wool, whilst his clothes seemed to be made of so rough a material, and were so ill-fitting that he resembled nothing so much as a Robinson Crusoe. It is related that once, when he was engaging a servant, the man stated as a reason for leaving his last situation that he failed to dress his master's hair to the latter's satisfaction. 'It is no object to me to have my hair dressed,' remarked Beethoven, as he signified his approval of the engagement. He always described himself as 'a disorderly creature,' and he certainly merited the designation. He was clumsy and awkward in his movements; he could not shave without cutting himself, or handle delicate things without breaking them; and whilst composing he invariably spilt the ink over the pianoforte. His handwriting was so illegible as to call forth objurgations from himself whenever he was called upon to decipher it. 'Yesterday,' he writes to a friend, 'I took a letter myself to the post office, and was asked where it was meant to go to; from which I see that my writing is as often misunderstood as I am myself.' Nevertheless, he was very fond of letter-writing, as the collections which have been preserved abundantly testify.

The letters of great men are often valued for the opinions

they contain on persons and subjects of the day, as well as for the insight they afford into the private thoughts and feelings of the writers. Beethoven's letters contain no word-pictures of scenery or events; nor do they express his views on questions or matters in which the world at large might be supposed to take an interest. But they are none the less valuable on that account; for they reflect the openness and simplicity of his character, and lay bare his wishes, his hopes and his disappointments, his joys and his sorrows—and especially his love of fun—just as one or another of these feelings or aspirations was uppermost at the moment.

As a teacher Beethoven exhibited none of the carelessness or impatience that characterised his personal habits. If the rendering of a passage was not in accordance with his own ideas of what it should be, he insisted upon the pupil playing it over and over again until he was satisfied. He was comparatively indifferent to the playing of wrong notes, but failure on the part of a pupil to give the right shade of expression, or to grasp the true character of a piece, never failed to arouse his anger. The one, he would say, might be an accident, but the other showed a want of knowledge, or feeling, or attention.

Beethoven was by nature exceedingly unpunctual, and frequently kept his pupils waiting for their lessons. Even Madame von Breuning, for whom he had a strong affection, and who was one of the few people who could be said to have managed him, often failed in persuading him to be in time. 'Ah! I may not disturb him—he is in his *raptus*,' she would exclaim despairingly, in allusion to his habit of relapsing into gloomy reverie. And not even his dearest friend dared to intrude upon him at such moments. His absent-mindedness was the subject of many a joke. He often forgot to come home to dinner—a fact which, seeing that he was a man, deserves to be recorded; and it is even said that, on one occasion, he insisted on tendering money for a meal which he had not ordered, under the belief that he had dined. At another time he composed a set of variations on a Russian dance for the wife of an officer in the Russian service—a compliment which was acknowledged by the gift of a horse. Straightway Beethoven forgot all about the horse until he was reminded of its existence by a long bill presented for its keep. He persisted in shaving himself at his bedroom window, without a blind, and exposed to the view of passers-by; and when he discovered that this habit caused a crowd of jeering idlers to collect in front of the house, he flew into a rage, and exchanged his lodgings for others situated in a more retired spot, rather than discontinue the practice. His explosive temper has furnished many amusing anecdotes. One day his cook, who, in consideration of her master's incurable unpunctuality, must be regarded as an aggrieved personage, served up some eggs which were not to his taste, and he emphasised his displeasure by throwing the entire batch at the head of the unfortunate domestic. On another occasion a waiter who mistook his order was rewarded by having the contents of a dish of stew poured over his head. Even where his temper was not concerned his manners were directly opposed to those prevailing in polite society—though, in a large measure, this may have been due to his perfect simplicity and his ignorance of what was expected of him. Thus, it is told that, returning from one of his long walks in the pouring rain, he would make straight for the sitting-room of the house in which he happened to be staying and calmly proceed to shake the water from his hat over the carpet and chairs, after the fashion of a retriever just emerged from a pond, humming to himself the while some theme which had been occupying his thoughts during his walk. One of his pleasanter habits, to which he was greatly attached, was washing. He would pour the water backwards and forwards over his hands with childish delight, and if, as frequently happened, a musical idea suggested itself to him during the operation, he became oblivious to everything else, and would continue to send the water to and fro, spilling it in huge quantities, until the floor resembled a miniature lake.

Beethoven would never allow that his disorderliness was

anything more than personal, always contending that he had a love of order and neatness with regard to his surroundings and arrangements. Yet here is a sketch of the condition of his living-room, as seen by one of his friends: "The most exquisite confusion reigned in his house. Books and music were scattered in all directions; here the residue of a cold luncheon, there some full, some half-emptied, bottles. On the desk the hasty sketch of a new quartet; in another corner the remains of a breakfast. On the pianoforte the scribbled hints for a noble symphony, yet little more than in embryo; hard by a proof-sheet, waiting to be returned; letters from friends, and on business, spread all over the floor. Between the windows a goodly Stracchino cheese, and on one side of it ample vestiges of a genuine Verona Salami....' If an article were missing Beethoven would declare that he knew just where to put his hand upon it; and then, when two or three days' search failed to discover its whereabouts, he would storm at the servants, asseverating that they hid his things away on purpose to annoy him. But the storm would clear as quickly as it had gathered, and peace reign once more, until the next occasion called it forth; and the servants knew their master's heart too well to be angered by his reproaches.

The mention of his rambles in the rain recalls his fondness for the open air. It was a passion which clung to him through life. As each summer came round, during these years of unremitting toil, he would hail with delight the moment when he could close the door of his lodgings in the hot, stuffy city, and betake himself to some retired spot where he could ramble about and hold communion with Nature, secure from interruption. 'No man,' he wrote to one of his friends, 'loves the country more. Woods, trees, and rocks give the response which man requires.... Every tree seems to say, "Holy, holy."' A forest was to him a paradise. He would penetrate its cool depths, and, selecting a tree which offered a seat in a forking branch close to the ground, he would climb into it and sit there for hours, buried in thought. It was amidst the trees of Schönbrunn that he made the first rough notes for several of his great works. With his back planted against the trunk of a favourite lime-tree, his legs stretched along the big branch, and his gaze fixed upon the network of branchlets and quivering leaves above him, he sketched the framework of the oratorio 'The Mount of Olives,' the opera 'Fidelio' (or 'Leonore,' as it was first called), and that glorious symphony which is known by the title of the 'Eroica.'

When not resting amidst the trees Beethoven would set off on long walks through the fields, sketch-book[5] in hand, and humming or roaring to himself as he went along. The rough jottings in the sketch-books were later on developed with the utmost care, being written out again and again, with fresh alterations and additions each time, until every trace of crudeness had disappeared, and the finished work stood out with such clearness and precision as to suggest that it had been but that moment created. Nothing, indeed, has struck those who have followed the gradual development of his work from the first sketches which have been preserved more than the number of attempts which mark the growth of the idea in the composer's mind, until it assumed its final form. Yet there was no trace in the finished work of the process of refining and elaboration through which it had passed.

Very curious was the origin of some of the suggestions which found their way into the sketch-books. It was Beethoven's practice to keep one of these books by his bedside, in case an idea occurred to him during the night, and it is told that he was once aroused by the knocking of a neighbour who had been accidentally locked out of his house in the small hours of the morning. The irate neighbour knocked four raps at a time, with a pause at the end of every fourth rap, and the rhythmic regularity of the sounds not only startled Beethoven out of his sleep, but suggested a musical idea to his mind. Up jumped the composer, and down went the idea in his sketch-book, and the next morning the jotting was included in one of his most striking compositions—the 'Violin Concerto in D,' where the passage, given to the drums, is many times repeated.

A village which formed one of his favourite resorts was Heiligenstadt, situated about seven miles from Vienna. Here he went in the summer of 1802, after a severe illness. For some time past he had been suffering from increasing deafness, and the malady seemed now to have reached an acute stage, so that his country surroundings failed to exercise their accustomed charm, and he fell into a deep melancholy. Indeed, he appeared to have become impressed with the idea that his life-work was ended, and that he had nothing to look forward to but the companionship of an affliction which must sever him from the social intercourse in which he delighted, and render his remaining years solitary and miserable. It would be difficult to imagine a more terrible calamity than that which had befallen Beethoven, or to exaggerate its effects upon an over-sensitive nature such as he possessed. As his deafness increased, his efforts to conceal the results of the malady from those outside his own immediate circle became more and more painfully evident. No one failed to observe how he was affected, yet none dared to commiserate with him; and when he discovered that his mistakes were drawing public attention to what he was so anxious to hide, his mortification was intensified to a degree that for the time destroyed his peace of mind and left him a prey to melancholy. It was whilst in this state of mental and physical depression that he penned from his village retreat the touchingly eloquent letter which has since been called his 'will.' In this epistle, which is addressed to 'My brothers Carl and Johann Beethoven,' and which they are admonished to 'read and execute after my demise,' Beethoven pleads for consideration both on account of his irritability and his apparent lack of affection. To his misfortunes, not to his faults, must be attributed the obstinacy, the hostility, or the misanthropic attitude which he has shown towards those whom he loves, and by whom he is loved in return. 'My heart and my mind,' he says, as if in extenuation of this fancied ill-feeling, 'were from childhood prone to the tender feelings of affection.' It is a pathetic appeal to natures which, unfortunately for the writer, were the least likely to echo its tenderness in their own hearts; for neither of the brothers had ever shown him true affection. They had followed him to Vienna to found a livelihood for themselves, and thenceforward, with selfish zeal for their own interests, they had simply served to clog his progress. Blinded by the nobility of his own character, however, Beethoven now takes upon himself the entire blame for what he imagines to be a lessening of the affection between them, and, sunk in health, and viewing his future through the darkest of glasses, he reproaches himself for what he could never have helped. Though his brothers are the only persons who are actually named in this remarkable letter, no one who reads it can doubt that Beethoven is addressing the world at large, who will judge both himself and his works.

Towards the end of this year his health had improved, but the deafness remained constant, and he was at length compelled to desist from conducting his works. Shortly after this an incident occurred which must have served to convince him of the sympathy which the public felt for him in his affliction. His great work, the 'Choral Symphony,' was being performed, and the composer was standing on the platform with his back to the audience, intently following the music. As the concluding chords died away the whole house broke out into enthusiastic applause. Again and again the shouts rent the air, but Beethoven stood motionless, unmoved—a pathetic figure amidst the storm. Possibly at this moment those whose ears he had charmed by his music realised to the full the ineffable sadness of his condition, for a reverential hush fell suddenly on the gathering. The next moment, however, the storm of cheers broke out afresh, for a young singer, named Caroline Unger, who had been taking part in the symphony, went up to the unconscious composer, and, taking his hand, turned him round to the audience. As the glance of the deaf man lighted upon the sea of upturned faces, and he witnessed the emotion which his work had aroused, he was deeply moved.

The 'Choral Symphony' ranks amongst the greatest of Beethoven's works, but we should like to mention one of his smaller, though not less famous, compositions—that which is known by the title of the 'Kreutzer Sonata for Pianoforte and Violin'—because no fitter illustration could be found of the rapidity with which the composer worked under pressure than is afforded by the beautiful work which he dedicated to his friend Rodolphe Kreutzer, a violinist attached to Count Bernadotte's suite of performers. He had undertaken the writing of the sonata at the instance of a violinist, a mulatto named Bridgetower, who was staying in Vienna, and it was to be jointly performed by Bridgetower and himself. The concert was announced to begin at 8 a.m., but when the public were hastening to the theatre in the Augarten at that early hour of the spring morning, the music for the pianoforte part was practically unwritten, with the exception of a few scattered suggestions, whilst the variations, which are justly renowned for their grace and beauty, were hurriedly written in at the last moment, and had to be played by the violinist at sight from the rough manuscript. The *andante* is of unsurpassable beauty, and it was rendered by the composer in such a manner as to excite the audience to enthusiasm. Beethoven's powers of playing were never shown to greater advantage than in his *andante* movements. His execution of the quicker parts was apt to be confused by his frequent use of the pedal, but nothing occurred to mar or obscure the clearness and depth of expression with which he rendered the slower movements, and it was in these that his playing was most truly inspired.

The year 1804 is a memorable one in the life of Beethoven, for it witnessed the completion of his grand symphony, the 'Eroica,' the rough idea of which had been sketched amidst the woods of Schönbrunn two years before. The suggestion of the work is said to have come from Count Bernadotte, the French Ambassador at Vienna, with whom Beethoven was on terms of intimacy; but the man whom it was intended to honour by its dedication was the General whose exploits had shaken the whole of Europe— Napoleon Buonaparte. Beethoven had been greatly attracted by Napoleon's character. He believed in him as the one man who was capable of making his adopted country a pattern for the world, by establishing a Republic on the principles laid down by Plato. But his confidence in the unselfishness of Napoleon's aims was soon to receive a rude shock. The fair copy of the symphony, with its dedicatory inscription, had been completed, and was on the point of being dispatched to Paris, when suddenly the news reached Vienna that the hero's glorious entry into the French capital had culminated in his allowing himself to be proclaimed Emperor. In a moment Beethoven's worship was turned into hatred and contempt. He seized the manuscript, tore the title-page to shreds, and flung the work itself to the other end of the room. 'He designs to become a tyrant, like the rest,' he exclaimed, with scornful bitterness; and it was a long time before he could even be induced to look at the music again, or to consider the question of its publication. Eventually, however, he consented to its appearing under a new title, the 'Sinfonia Eroica,' by which it has since been known to the world.

It is impossible within the limits of a short story-life to give even a brief description of the composer's chief works, or to convey more than an idea of how much work, despite his irregular habits, Beethoven accomplished. His untiring industry in developing the rough jottings which formed the foundations of his compositions has been mentioned; but without following his life from year to year we can have only a very imperfect conception of the actual amount of labour which was involved in bringing to perfection the long list of works that we see appended to the biographies of the composer. When we follow the story of his life in detail, we are struck by the fact of his unceasing toil. Nothing seems to have checked the constant flow of composition; yet many causes were at work to hinder it, such as ill-health, poverty, an ill-balanced temperament, and an oversensitiveness with regard to the petty troubles arising out of his injudicious mode of life. 'I live only in my music,' he writes, 'and no sooner is one thing done than the next is begun. As I am now writing, I often work at three or four things at once.' And think what such work meant! It has been said that it is difficult to find in Beethoven's life anything corresponding to the extraordinary beauty and grandeur of his creations—in other words, there seems to exist no parallel in his life, as he lived it, to the outpourings of his musical soul. There is, indeed, little doubt that Beethoven had but one channel through which to express his deepest thoughts and feelings—the language of music. Through his music he reaches our hearts; by his music we are brought into contact with his innermost soul; and by his music alone can we know the man Beethoven as he really was.

Yet his life was by no means devoid of noble qualities. It was in every sense a great life, full of energy, full of power, full of a determination which carried him through every obstacle, and enabled him to hold his own against the attacks of his enemies. Apart, however, from the genius that ennobled it, it was not a life which could altogether compel admiration. The downright simplicity and directness of purpose which shone forth as Beethoven's chief characteristics, and in themselves were undoubted virtues, were, unhappily, overshadowed by faults and shortcomings of such magnitude as to shut out much of the friendship and sympathy that he might otherwise have enjoyed; and no one reading his life can doubt that he stood greatly in need of such assistance.

Nevertheless, Beethoven's faults were of the head, not of the heart. At heart he was a man capable of loving and worthy to be loved. His simple nature was easily touched by distress, and just as easily imposed upon by those who designed to use him for their own ends. Many of his quarrels and dislikes were either brought about or fomented by persons in whom he had placed a mistaken faith. This was notably the case with regard to the quarrel with Stephen Breuning, his best and truest friend, to whom, after a separation of years, he turned with an appeal for pardon that did honour to his heart. The letter accompanied a miniature of the composer, and ran as follows:

'Beneath this portrait, dear Stephen, may all that has for so long gone on between us be for ever hidden. I know how I have torn your heart. For this the emotion that you must certainly have noticed in me has been sufficient punishment. My feeling towards you was not malice. No—I should no longer be worthy of your friendship; it was passionate love for you and myself; but I doubted you dreadfully, for people came between us who were unworthy of us both. My portrait has long been intended for you. I need not tell you that I never meant it for anyone else. Who could I give it to with my warmest love so well as to you, true, good, noble Stephen? Forgive me for distressing you. I have suffered myself as much as you have. It was only when I had you no longer with me that I first really felt how dear you are, and always will be, to my heart. Come to my arms once more, as you used to do.'

Carl, the brother in whose unworthy behalf Beethoven had taken up the cudgels against his best friend, was dead when this touching appeal was written, but he had bequeathed to Beethoven a solemn charge which was destined to bring to him who undertook it in the goodness of his heart a burden of sorrow and bitterness. Carl had died penniless, and his boy, who bore the father's name, thenceforth became to his Uncle Ludwig as his own son. How good, how generous and self-sacrificing Beethoven was to his nephew is testified by all who have written of his life. He supplied him freely with money when money was by no means too plentiful; he strove to satisfy his every need, either fancied or real; and he lavished upon him a great love and solicitude to the last day of his life. But Carl showed himself to be utterly unworthy of this affection. He treated his uncle shamefully, and instead of endeavouring to repay his kindness by steady perseverance, he was a disgrace to the family whose name he bore. There is, unfortunately, only too much reason for believing that Carl's want of affection, coupled with his dissolute habits, embittered his uncle's existence, estranged him from his friends, and hurried on his death.

Of Beethoven's tenderness of heart numerous instances are recorded. He devoted much of his time to arranging concerts for the benefit of the poor and suffering, and in the midst of his popularity and the heavy demands upon his time and strength he always found a means of helping others. When he first came to Vienna to reside, he made the acquaintance of a musician named Förster, from whom he received instruction in the art of quartet writing. Beethoven never forgot this kindly help, and long afterwards, when Förster was living in the upper part of his house, he gave music-lessons to his friend's little six-year-old boy. The lessons could only be given before breakfast, and as Beethoven was an early riser, the boy had to get up in the dark on those winter mornings and go down to the practice-room. May we not picture for ourselves the little child seated beside the grave composer in the dimly-lighted room, striving with chilly fingers to find the right notes, whilst the master, bending over him, sets him right with a tenderness which no one else is near to witness?

'I feel as if I had written scarcely more than a few notes,' were the words used by Beethoven in writing to a friend in 1824, when he was near the close of his full and eventful life; and they serve to show how exhaustless was that energy which neither sorrow nor disease had the power to repress. Still, he yearns to 'bring a few great works into the world, and then,' he adds, 'like an old child, to end my earthly course somewhere amongst good people.' These latter years had, indeed, been very full ones, both of work and anxieties, and the inroads of disease had been steadily undermining his strength. Yet the picture which is given to us of the composer when within a few months of his death is a vivid portrayal of the triumph of mind-force over physical weakness. He was staying in the country, at the house of his brother Johann, and the picture of his daily life there is drawn by the hand of his serving-man. 'At half-past five he was up and at his table, beating time with hands and feet, singing, humming, and writing. At half-past seven was the family breakfast, and directly after it he hurried out of doors, and would saunter about the fields, calling out, waving his hands, going now very slowly, then very fast, and then suddenly standing still and writing in a kind of pocket-book. At half-past twelve he came into the house to dinner, and after dinner he went to his own room till three or so; then again in the fields till about sunset, for later than that he might not go out. At half-past seven was supper, and then he went to his room, wrote till ten, and so to bed.'

One more picture, and our story ends. Beethoven was lying on his death-bed when the news was brought to him that Hummel, the musician, with whom he had been intimate in the old Vienna days, had just arrived in the city. Many years had elapsed since Beethoven had severed his friendship with Hummel in a sudden fit of pique, and there had been no attempt at reconciliation. But now, wasted by disease, and fast sinking into his grave, there was no room in his heart for aught but joy at the knowledge that one whom he had formerly liked was so near him. 'Oh,' he cried, raising himself in bed when he heard the news—'oh, if he would but call to see me!' No one seems to have carried the message from the dying man, but it was answered. A few days later Hummel came, and the old friends were at once in each other's arms. Hummel, struck by the terrible signs of suffering in Beethoven's face, broke into bitter weeping. Beethoven tried to calm him, and, pulling from beneath his pillow a sketch of Haydn's birthplace which he had that morning received, he cried, 'Look, my dear Hummel, here is Haydn's birthplace! So great a man born in so mean a cottage!'

Beethoven died on March 26, 1827, having recently completed

his fifty-sixth year. Two days before his death he received the last Sacraments of the Church. 'As the evening closed in, at a quarter to six, there came a sudden storm of hail and snow, covering the ground and roofs of the Schwarzspanierplatz, and followed by a flash of lightning and an instant clap of thunder. So great was the crash as to rouse even the dying man. He opened his eyes, clenched his fist, and shook it in the air above him. This lasted a few seconds, while the hail rushed down outside, and then the hand fell, and the great composer was no more.'[6]

On March 29, at three o'clock in the afternoon, Beethoven was laid to rest in the Währinger Cemetery, Vienna. The funeral was a very grand one. Twenty thousand people followed him to his grave, and soldiers were needed to force a way for the coffin through the densely packed mass awaiting its arrival at the cemetery gates. Amongst the mourners was Schubert, the composer, who had visited him on his death-bed, and who acted as one of the torch-bearers. A choir of men singers and trombones performed and sang several of the master's compositions, as the great procession wended its way to the graveside, and Hummel laid three wreaths of laurel upon the coffin before it was lowered to its resting-place.

FOOTNOTES:

[1] Mozart had died in December of the previous year.

[2] Schindler, 'Life of Beethoven.'

[3] Moscheles, in Schindler's 'Life of Beethoven.'

[4] Sir G. Grove, 'Dictionary of Music and Musicians.'

[5] One of these sketch-books, filled with his notes, is to be seen in the Manuscript Room of the British Museum.

[6] Sir G. Grove, 'Dictionary of Music and Musicians.'

A CHAPTER FROM
Story-Lives of Great Musicians, 1907

A SKETCH OF BEETHOVEN

A LECTURE

By Thomas Hanly Ball

OVERTURE

"Give me sweet music when I'm glad
Give me sweet music when I'm sad;
For music softens every woe,
And brightens every rapture's flow.

"Oh! give me music! In my years
Of childhood's hopes and childhood's fears,
One sweetly-breathing vocal lay
Could steal my griefs, my fears away.

"Yes, music, come! Thou dying voice
Of distant days—of far-past joys—
Come, softly breathe into mine ear,
And thine shall be the flowing tear!

"Come in the strain I loved so well,
And of the lip that breathed it tell.
Oh! be the lingerings of thy lays
The voice of those departed days!"

Association not only gives significancy to music, but contributes greatly to heighten its agreeable effect. We have heard it performed, some time or other, in an agreeable place, perhaps, or by an agreeable person, or accompanied with words that describe agreeable ideas; or we have heard it in our early years—a period of life which we seldom look back upon without pleasure, and of which Bacon recommends the frequent recollection, as an expedient to preserve health. Nor is it necessary that musical compositions should have much intrinsic merit, or that they should call up any distinct remembrance of the agreeable ideas associated with them. There are seasons at which we are gratified with very moderate excellence. In childhood every tune is delightful to a musical ear: in our advanced years, an indifferent tune will[55] please, when set off by the amiable qualities of the performer, or by any other agreeable circumstance. The flute of a shepherd, heard at a distance, on a fine summer day, amidst beautiful scenery, will give rapture to the wanderer, though the tune, the instrument, and the musician be such as he could not endure in any other place. If a song, or piece of music, should call up only a faint remembrance that we were happy the last time we heard it, nothing more would be needful to make us listen to it again with peculiar satisfaction.

Well has Cowper said—

> "There is in souls a sympathy with sounds;
> And as the mind is pitch'd, the ear is pleased
> With melting airs, or martial, brisk or grave,
> Some chord in unison with what we hear
> Is touched within us, and the heart replies.
> How soft the music of those village bells,
> Falling at intervals upon the ear
> In cadence sweet, now dying all away,
> Now pealing loud again, and louder still,
> Clear and sonorous, as the gale comes on!
> With easy force it opens all the cells

Where mem'ry slept. Wherever I have heard
A kindred melody, the scene recurs,
And with it all its pleasures and its pains."

Of its influence very many anecdotes, I should rather say, *facts* are recorded.

Naturalists assert that animals and birds are sensible to the charms of music—take one or two instances:—

An officer was confined in the Bastile; he begged the governor to permit him the use of his lute, to soften by the harmonies of his instrument, the rigours of his prison. At the end of a few days, this modern Orpheus, playing on his lute, was greatly astonished to see frisking out of their holes, great numbers of *mice*, and descending from their woven habitations crowds of *spiders*, who formed a circle about him, while he continued breathing his soul-subduing instrument. He was petrified with astonishment. Having ceased to play, the assembly who did not come to see him, but to hear his instrument, immediately broke up. As he had a great dislike to spiders, it was two days before he ventured again to touch his instrument. At length, having overcome, for the novelty of his company, his dislike of them, he recommenced his concert, when the assembly was by far more numerous than at first; and in the course of further time, he found himself surrounded by a hundred *musical amateurs*. Having thus succeeded in attracting this company, he treacherously contrived to get rid of them at his will. For this purpose he begged the keeper to give him a cat, which he put in a cage, and let loose at the very instant when the little hairy people were most enchanted by the Orphean skill he displayed.

Haydyn tells the following story:—

"I went, with some other young people equally devoid of care, one day during the extreme heat of summer, to seek for coolness and fresh air on one of the lofty mountains, which surround the Lago Maggiore in Lombardy. Having reached by daybreak the middle of the ascent,[58] we stopped to contemplate

133

the Borromean isles, which were displayed under our feet, in the middle of the lake, when we were surrounded by a large flock of sheep, which were leaving the fold to go to their pasture.

One of our party, who was no bad performer on the flute, and who always carried his instrument along with him, took it out of his pocket. "I am going," said he, "to turn Corydon; let us see whether Virgil's sheep will recognize their pastor." He began to play. The sheep and goats, which were following one another towards the mountain, with their heads hanging down, raised them at the first sound of the flute, and all with a general and hasty movement turned to the side from whence the agreeable noise proceeded. Gradually they flocked round the musician, and listened with motionless attention. He ceased playing; still the sheep did not stir. The shepherd with his staff, obliged those nearest to him to move on; they obeyed; but no sooner did the fluter begin to play, than his innocent audience again returned to him. The shepherd, out of patience, pelted them with clods of earth; but not one would move. The fluter played with additional skill. The shepherd fell into a passion, whistled, scolded, and pelted the poor fleecy amateurs with stones. Such as were hit by them began to march; but the others still refused to stir."

Marville gives us the following curious account:—

"Doubting the truth of those who say that the love of music is a natural taste, especially the sound of instruments, and that beasts themselves are touched by it; being one day in the country, I tried an experiment.

While a man was playing on the trump marine, I made my observations on a *cat*, a *dog*, a *horse*, an *ass*, a *hind*, *cows*, *small birds*, and a *cock and hens*, who were in a yard, under a window on which I was leaning.

I did not perceive that the *cat* was the least affected, and I even judged by her air that she would have given all the instruments in the world for a mouse, sleeping in the sun all the time.

The *horse* stopped short from time to time before the window, raising his head up now and then, as he was feeding on the grass.

The *dog* continued for above an hour seated on his hind legs, looking steadfastly at the player.

The *ass* did not discover the least indication of his being touched, eating his thistles peaceably.

The *hind* lifted up her large, wide ears, and seemed very attentive.

The *cows* slept a little, and after gazing, as though they had been acquainted with us, went forward.

Some *little birds*, who were in an aviary, and others on the trees and bushes, almost tore their little throats with singing.

But the *cock*, who minded only his hens, and the hens, who were solely employed in scratching a neighbouring dunghill, did not show in any manner that they took the least pleasure in hearing the trump marine."

One of the best descriptions of the influence of music I consider to be Wordsworth's lines on the Blind Fiddler of Oxford Street. Many of you, doubtless, are familiar with them; but for the information of those who may not, I shall quote them.

"An Orpheus! an Orpheus! Yes, faith may grow bold,
And take to herself all the wonders of old.
Near the stately Pantheon you'll meet with the same
In the street that from Oxford hath borrowed its name.

"His station is there, and he works on the crowd:
He sways them with harmony merry and loud:
He fills with his power all their hearts to the brim.
Was aught ever heard like his fiddle and him?

"What an eager assembly! what an empire is this!
The weary have life, and the hungry have bliss;
The mourner is cheered, and the anxious have rest;
And the guilt-burthened soul is no longer opprest.

"As the moon brightens round her the clouds of the night,
So he, where he stands, is a centre of light;
It gleams on the face there of dusk-browed Jack
And the pale-visaged bakers, with basket on back.

"That errand-bound 'prentice was passing in haste—
What matter! he's caught—and his time runs to waste;
The newsman is stopped, though he stops on the fret;
And the half-breathless lamplighter he's in the net!

"The porter sits down on the weight which he bore;
The lass with her barrow wheels hither her store
If a thief could be here, he might pilfer at ease:
She sees the musician—'tis all that she sees!

"That tall man, a giant in bulk and in height,
Not an inch of his body is free from delight.
Can he keep himself still, if he would? Oh not he!
The music stirs in him, like wind through a tree.

"Mark that cripple, who leans on his crutch, like a tower
That long has leaned forward, leans hour after hour!
That mother, whose spirit in fetters is bound,
While she dandles the babe in her arms to the sound.

"Now coaches and chariots roar on like a stream;
Here are twenty souls happy as souls in a dream;
They are deaf to your murmurs—they care not for you,
Nor what ye plying, nor what ye pursue!

"He stands, backed by the wall—he abates not his din;
His hat gives him vigour, with boons dropping in
From the old and the young—from
   the poorest; and there—
The one-pennied boy has his penny to spare!

"Oh! blest are the hearers! and proud be the hand
Of the pleasure it spreads through so thankful a band!
I'm glad for him, blind as he is! All the while,
If they speak 'tis to praise, and they praise with a smile."

But why should I occupy your time by quotations from celebrated poets or prose writers, to prove the influence of music, when I have it in my power to verify the saying of that eminent composer whose life I have undertaken to sketch?

"The effect of music on a man should be to strike fire from his soul."

SONATA PATHETIQUE

Ludwig Von Beethoven was born on the 17th December, 1770, at Bonn. His father and grandfather were both musicians by profession. The former occupied the situation of principal vocal tenor, and the latter that of first bass singer in the chapel of the Elector of Cologne.

From the earliest age Beethoven evinced a disposition for music; or, in other words, he learnt the language of music and his mother tongue both at the same time; and as modulated sounds seldom fail to make a deep impression on a young, fervid mind, when they are almost constantly presented to it, as was the case in the present instance, he soon acquired, and as speedily manifested, a taste for the art of which they are the foundation.

His father began to instruct him when he was only in his fifth year. An anecdote is told of his early performances, which corroborates what I have already said on the influence of music. It is said that, whenever little Ludwig was playing in his closet on the violin, a spider would let itself down from the ceiling and alight upon the instrument. The story, I am sorry, goes on to say that his mother one day, discovering her son's companion, destroyed it, whereupon little Ludwig dashed his violin to shatters.

At the early age of thirteen, Beethoven published at Mannheim, in his own name, Variations on a March, Sonatas, and Songs. But at this time his genius displayed itself more decidedly in musical improvisations. His extempore fantasias are mentioned by Gerber, in his Lexicon, as having excited the admiration of the most accomplished musicians of the time.

The fame of his youthful genius attracted the attention of the Elector of Cologne, who sent him at his own expense to Vienna, in character of his Court organist, to study under the celebrated Haydyn, in order to perfect himself in the art of composition.

Vienna was at this time (1792), the central point of every thing great and sublime, that music had till then achieved on the soil of Germany.

Mozart, the source of all light in the region of harmony, whose acquaintance Beethoven had made on his first visit to Vienna in 1786, who when he heard Beethoven extemporize upon a theme that was given him, exclaimed to those present, "This youth will some day make a noise in the world"—Mozart, though he had been a year in his grave, yet lived freshly in the memory of all who had a heart susceptible of his divine revelations, as well as in Beethoven's. Gluck's spirit still hovered around the inhabitants of the old city—F. Haydyn and many other distinguished men in every art, and in every branch of human knowledge, yet lived and worked together harmoniously. In short, no sooner had Beethoven, then but twenty-two, looked around him in this favoured abode of the Muses, and made a few acquaintances, than he said to himself, "Here will I stay, and not return to Bonn even though the Elector should cut off my pension."

Beethoven did not long enjoy the instructions of his master, for Haydyn handed him over to the care and instructions of the learned Allrechtsberger. It appears, that the character of Beethoven was marked by great singularity from his earliest years. Both Haydyn and Allrechtsberger, but particularly the latter, have recorded that he was not willing to profit by good advice. Beethoven has himself been heard to confess, that among other peculiarities which he prided himself on displaying, when a young man, was that of refusing to acknowledge himself as the pupil of Haydyn, at which this master took great offence.

The consequence of this self-confident spirit was, that at this period, he made but little progress in composition, and was more ambitious to become a brilliant performer. Hence by the periodicals of that day, he is not allowed to possess the ability of composition; harshness of modulation, melodies more singular than pleasing, and a constant struggle to be original, are among the principal faults of which he was accused. As to the latter charge it may be remarked, that it is the besetting sin which has adhered to Beethoven through life; and who can help wishing that with it, he had also possessed the power of spreading the vice among his contemporaries, and of bequeathing it to his successors. But if this indefatigable search after originality be a sin, to what new and extraordinary effects, to what wonders, has it not given birth? To whom so justly than to this author can these lines be applied—

> "Great wits may sometimes gloriously offend,
> And rise to faults true critics dare not mend?"

Beethoven never defended himself against criticisms or attacks, he never suffered them to have more than a superficial effect upon him. Not indifferent to the opinions of the good, he took no notice of the attacks of the malicious, and allowed them to go on unchecked, even when they proceeded so far as to assign him a place, sometimes in one madhouse, sometimes in another. "If it *amuses* people to say or to write such stuff concerning me, let them continue so to do as long as they please."

(This may remind you of an anecdote of the Earl of Derby; being once attacked in the House of Lords by the Duke of Argyle, the Earl in his reply said, "A certain navvy, who happened to be married to a very violent woman, a regular virago, was asked why he allowed his wife to abuse him, or use such intemperate language. 'Poor creature,' said the navvy, 'it amuses her, and does not hurt me.' So say I, the attack of the noble duke may amuse him but cannot injure me.")

As in that classic period of musical activity, Beethoven was the sun which all strove to approach, and rejoiced if they could but catch a glance of his brilliant eyes, it was natural that he should converse much with ladies, several of whom were always contending for his affections at once, as it is well known, and he more than once found himself like Hercules in a dilemma. Dr. Wegeler, in his life of Beethoven says, "He was never without an attachment, and that mostly he was very deeply smitten." This is quite true. How could any rational person who is acquainted with Beethoven, or ever heard his compositions, maintain the contrary. Whoever is capable of feeling how powerfully the pure flame of love operates upon the imagination, more especially of the sensitive and highly endowed artist, and how in all his productions it goes before him like a light sent down from Heaven to guide him, will take it for granted without any evidence that Beethoven was susceptible of the purest love, and that he was conducted by it. What genius could have composed the Fantasia in C, commonly called the "Moonlight or the Moonshine Sonata," without such a passion? It was love, for Bettine, to whom that imaginative composition is dedicated, (and to whom I shall again have occasion to allude,) which inspired him while engaged upon it. This piece will now be performed, and judge for yourselves whether I have said too much in its praise:—

Fantasia in C., commonly called the "Moonlight Sonata," to designate this enthusiastic period of Beethoven's passion.

In the year 1800, we find Beethoven engaged in the

composition of his "Christ on the Mount of Olives." He wrote this work during his summer residence at Hetzendorf, a pleasant village, closely contiguous to the gardens of the imperial palace of Shönbrunn, where he passed several summers of his life in profound seclusion. A circumstance connected with this great work, and of which Beethoven many years afterwards still retained a lively recollection, was that he composed it in the thickest part of the wood, in the park of Shönbrunn, seated between the two stems of an oak, which shot out from the main trunk at the height of about two feet from the ground.

About this period Beethoven endured much family annoyance and domestic trouble. His brothers who had some years previously followed him to Vienna, began to govern him and to make him suspicious of his sincerest friends and adherents, from wrong notions or even from jealousy. Surrounded by friends who loved and esteemed him—his fame already established—with an ample income, he ought to have been completely happy; and he certainly would have been but for an infirmity which began to afflict him, and the persecution of his brothers. His misery both of mind and body, I can best describe by reading a portion of his extraordinary will, which he at this time executed, and having that song sung which he at the same time composed, with special reference to the torture he was undergoing.

EXTRACTS FROM BEETHOVEN'S WILL

"O ye who consider or declare me to be hostile, obstinate, or misanthropic, what injustice ye do me! Ye know not the secret causes of that which to you wears such an appearance. My heart and my mind were from childhood prone to the tender feelings of affection. Nay, I was always disposed even to perform great actions. Born, with a lively, ardent disposition, susceptible to the diversions of society, I was forced at an early age to renounce them and to pass my life in seclusion. If I strove at any time to set myself above all this, O, how cruelly was I driven back, by the doubly painful experience of my defective hearing! And yet it was not possible for me to say to people, 'Speak louder, for I am deaf.' Ah! how could I proclaim the defect of a sense, that I once possessed in the highest perfection, in a perfection in which few of my colleagues possess or ever did possess it? Indeed, I cannot. Forgive me then, if ye see me draw back when I would gladly mingle among you.

"O God, thou lookest down upon my misery; thou knowest that it is accompanied with love of my fellow creatures, and a disposition to do good! O, men, when ye shall read this, think that ye have wronged me!

I go to meet death with joy; if he comes before I have had occasion to develop all my professional abilities, he will come too soon for me, in spite of my hard fate, and I should wish that he had delayed his arrival. But even then I am content, for he will release me from a state of endless suffering. Come when thou wilt, I shall meet thee with firmness. Farewell."

> "There is a calm for those who weep;
> A rest for weary pilgrims found;
> And while the mouldering ashes sleep
>   Low in the ground,
> The soul of origin divine,
> God's glorious image, freed from day,
> In Heaven's eternal sphere shall shine
>   A star of day."

In Questa Tomba Oscura.
Words by Göthe; Music by Beethoven

Let us proceed from grave to gay. I have already told you that Beethoven was a man of ardent feeling, and passionately in love with a young lady, Madame Von Arnim. I will read to you, one of his love letters, and I recommend the style to all the unmarried I have the pleasure to address:—

VIENNA, *August 11th, 1810.*

"DEAREST BETTINE,

"Never was a fairer spring than this year's; this I say and feel, too, as in it I made your acquaintance. You must, indeed, have yourself seen, that, in society, I was like a fish cast on the sand, that writhes, and struggles, and cannot escape, until some benevolent Galatea helps back again into the mighty sea; in very truth, I was fairly aground. Dearest Bettine, unexpectedly I met you, and at a moment when chagrin had completely overcome me; but, truly, your aspect put it to flight. I was aware in an instant that you belong to a totally different world from this absurd one, to which, even with the best wish to be tolerant, it is impossible to open one's ears. I am myself a poor creature, and yet complain of others! this you will, however, forgive, *with the kindly heart that looks out from your eyes, and with the intelligence that dwells in your ears*—at least, your ears know how to flatter when they listen. Mine, alas! are a barrier through which I can have hardly any friendly intercourse with mankind, else, perhaps, I might have acquired a still more entire confidence in you. As it was, I could only comprehend the full, expressive glance of your eyes, and this has so moved me that I shall never forget it. Divine Bettine! dearest girl! Art! who comprehends the meaning of this word? With whom may I speak of this great divinity? how I love the recollections of the few days when we used to chat with each other, or rather correspond. I have preserved every one of the little scraps of paper on which your intelligent, precious, most precious replies were given—thus, at least, may I thank my worthless ears that the best portion of our fugitive discourse is retained in writing.

"Since you went, I have had many uncomfortable hours, in

which the power to do anything is lost. After you had gone away, I rambled about for some three hours in the Museum at Schönbrunn; but no good angel met me there, to chide me into good humour, as an angel like you might have done. Forgive, sweetest Bettine, this transition from the fundamental key—but I must have such intervals to vent my feelings.

"And you have written of me to Göethe, have you not? saying that I would fain pack up my head in a cask, where I should see nothing and hear nothing of what passes in the world, since you, dearest angel, meet me here no longer. But, surely I shall at least have a letter from you. Hope supports me—she is, indeed, the nursing mother of half the world, and she has been my close friend all my life long—what would have become of me else? I send with this 'Knowest thou the land,' which I have just composed, as a memorial of the time when I first became acquainted with you."

This song will now be sung for you. The words are from the German of Göthe.

"Knowest thou the land where the sweet citron blows."

Beethoven's interviews with Bettine were not all wasted in rhapsodies of love. In one of his conversations with this accomplished lady he thus eloquently describes the power of poetry and the philosophy of music:—

"Göthe's poems exercise a great sway over me, not only by their meaning but by their rhythm also. It is a language that urges me on to composition, that builds up its own lofty standard, containing in itself all the mysteries of harmony, so that I have but to follow up the radiations of that centre from which melodies evolve spontaneously. I pursue them eagerly, overtake them, then again see them flying before me, vanish in the multitude of my impressions, until I seize them anew with increased vigour no more to be parted from them. It is then that my transports give them every diversity of modulation: it is I who triumph over the first of these musical thoughts, and the shape I give it I call symphony. Yes, Bettina, *music is the link between intellectual and sensual life.*

"Melody gives a sensible existence to poetry; for does not the meaning of a poem become embodied in melody? The mind would embrace all thoughts, both high and low, and embody them into one stream of sensations, all sprung from simple melody, and without the aid of its charms doomed to die in oblivion. This is the unity which lives in my symphonies—numberless streamlets meandering on, in endless variety of shape, but all diverging into one common bed. Thus it is I feel that there is an indefinite something, an eternal, an infinite to be attained; and although I look upon my works with a foretaste of success, yet I cannot help wishing, like a child, to begin my task anew, at the very moment that my thundering appeal to my hearers seems to have forced my musical creed upon them, and thus to have exhausted the insatiable cravings of my soul after my 'beau ideal.'

"Music alone ushers man into the portal of an intellectual world, ready to encompass *him*, but which *he* may never encompass. That mind alone whose every thought is rhythm can embody music, can comprehend its mysteries, its divine inspirations, and can alone speak to the senses of its intellectual revelations. Although spirits may feed upon it as we do upon air, yet it may not nourish all mortal men; and those privileged few alone, who have drawn from its heavenly source, may aspire to hold spiritual converse with it. How few are these! for, like the thousands who marry for love, and who profess love, whilst love will single out but one amongst them, so also will thousands court Music, whilst she turns a deaf ear to all but the chosen few. She, too, like her sister arts, is based upon morality—*that fountain-head of genuine invention!* And would you know the true principle on which the arts *may* be won? It is to bow to their immutable terms, to lay all passion and vexation of spirit prostrate at [81]their feet, and to approach their divine presence with a mind so calm and so void of littleness as to be ready to receive the dictates of fantasy and the revelations of truth. Thus the art becomes a divinity, man approaches her with religious feelings, his inspirations are God's divine gifts, and his aim fixed by the same hand from above which helps him to attain it."

And he adds:—"We know not whence our knowledge is derived. The seeds which lie dormant in us require the dew, the warmth, and the electricity of the soil to spring up, to ripen into thought, and to break forth. Music is the electrical soil in which the mind thrives, thinks, and invents. Music herself teaches us harmony; for *one* musical thought bears upon the whole kindred of ideas, and each is linked to the other, closely and indissolubly, by the ties of harmony."

Hearken to proof of the truth of this eloquent and beautiful description of music.

WALTZ—BEETHOVEN

The talents of a Haydyn and Mozart raised instrumental composition in Germany to an astonishing elevation; and Beethoven may be said not only to have maintained the art in that stupendous altitude, but even in some respects to have brought it to a still higher degree of perfection. "Haydyn," says Reichardt, "drew his quartets from the pure source of his sweet and unsophisticated nature, his captivating simplicity and cheerfulness. In these works he is still without an equal. Mozart's mightier genius and richer imagination took a more extended range, and embodied in several passages the most profound and sublime qualities of his own mind. Moreover, he was much greater as a performer than Haydyn, and as such expected more from instruments than the latter did. He also allowed more merit to highly-wrought and complicated compositions, and thus raised a gorgeous palace within Haydyn's fairy bower. Of this palace Beethoven was an early inmate; and in order adequately to express his own peculiar forms of style, he had no other means but to surmount the edifice with that defying and colossal tower which no one will probably presume to carry higher with impunity.

"If any man," says an able writer in the Quarterly, "can be said to enjoy an almost universal admiration as composer, it is Beethoven—who, disdaining to copy his predecessors in any, the most distant manner, has, notwithstanding, by his energetic, bold, and uncommon style of writing, carried away a prize from our modern Olympus."

Beethoven, like most great men, had many peculiarities.

In winter, well as in summer, it was his practice to rise at daybreak, and immediately to sit down to his writing-table. There he would labour till two or three o'clock, his usual dinnertime. Scarcely had the last morsel been swallowed, when, if he had no more distant excursion in view, he took his usual walk—that is to say, he ran in double quick time, as if hunted by bailiffs, twice round the town—whether it rained,[84] or snowed, or hailed, or the thermometer stood an inch or two below the freezing point—whether Boreas blew a chilling blast from the Bohemian mountains, or whether the thunder roared, and forked lightnings played, what signified it to the enthusiastic lover of his art, in whose genial mind, perhaps, were budding, at that very moment, when the elements were in fiercest conflict, the harmonious feelings of a balmy spring.

The use of the bath was as much a necessity to Beethoven as to a Turk—and he was in the habit of submitting himself to frequent ablutions. When it happened that he did not walk out of doors to collect his ideas, he would, not unfrequently, in a fit of the most complete abstraction, go to his washhand basin, and pour several jugs of water upon his hands, all the time humming and roaring. After dabbling in the water till his clothes were wet through, he would pace up and down the room with a vacant expression of countenance, and his eyes distended, the singularity of his aspect being often increased by an unshaven beard. Then he would seat himself at his table and write; and afterwards get up again to the washhand basin and dabble and hum as before. Ludicrous as were these scenes, no one dared venture to notice them, or to disturb him while engaged in his inspiring ablutions, for these were his moments of profoundest meditation.

Many anecdotes are told of him likewise.

The wife of an esteemed pianoforte player, residing in Vienna, was a great admirer of Beethoven, and she earnestly wished to possess a lock of his hair—her husband, anxious to gratify her, applied to a gentleman who was very intimate with Beethoven, and who had rendered him some service. Beethoven sent the lady a lock of hair cut from a *goat's beard*—and Beethoven's own hair being very grey and harsh, there was no reason to fear that the hoax would be very readily detected. The lady was overjoyed at possessing this supposed memorial of her saint, proudly showing it to all her acquaintance; but, when her happiness at its height, some one who happened to know the secret, made her acquainted with the deception that had been practised on her—the lady's wrath who will attempt to describe?

Beethoven's name I have already told you was Ludwig Von Beethoven. In some legal proceedings in which he was concerned, it was intimated by the court that the word von, of Dutch origin, does not ennoble the family to whose name it is prefixed—according to the laws of Holland—that, in the province of the Rhine in which Beethoven was born, it was held to be of no higher value—that, consequently, the halo of nobility ought to be stripped from this Von in Austria also. Beethoven was accordingly required to produce proofs of his nobility. "My *nobility*! My *nobility*!" he exclaimed—"*Why, my nobility is here, here!*"—clapping his forehead.

Right, Beethoven, brains are the highest nobility, if not the richest. I love birth, and ancestry, when they are incentives to exertion not the title deeds to sloth. Who would not prefer being the descendant of a Stephenson, an Arkwright, or a

Crompton, or any other of those great architects of their own fortunes, and to feel some of their noble energies, firing their blood to efforts of industry, than to be for ever falling back on some legend or fiction of ancestry; and in the absence of any *personal* claim to greatness to be referring back and depending on those great mistakes of our forefathers, when he who waded through slaughter to a peerage was honoured *above* those whose brains and whose industry were the means of promoting the comfort of their fellow men. Believe me, my young friends, the highest honour of earth, is the honour of independence, and the highest nobility, *to be the Rodolph of your own fortune, and a benefactor to mankind.*

Beethoven died 26th March, 1827, in the fifty-sixth year of his age. Although his warmth[88] of temper, extreme frankness and singularity of manners, his little reserve in judging of people, and above all, that deplorable calamity—the greatest which can befall a man of his profession—his extreme deafness, seemed little calculated to endear him to the true admirers of his genius. Still, notwithstanding his foibles, which much more frequently belong to great than to ordinary men, his character as a man and as a citizen ranked deservedly high. Although his originality induced him to deviate from ordinary rules, in the little affairs of common life, yet his high feeling of honour and right produced a rectitude in his moral conduct, which ensured to him the esteem of every honourable man.

Beethoven—the master spirit of his age—
    Has passed away to his eternal rest,
His name belongs to history's page,
    Enrolled with men the noblest and the best.

We to whom it was not given to view
    His living lineaments with wond'ring eye,
May in his tones behold him pictured true
    In breathing colours that can never die.

For he could paint in tones of magic force
    The moody passions of the varying soul;
Now winding round the heart with playful course;
    Now storming all the breast with wild control.

Forthdrawing from his unexhausted store,
    'Twas his to bid the burden'd heart o'erflow,
Infusing joys it never knew before,
    And melting it with soft luxuriant woe!

He liveth! It is wrong to say he's dead—
    The sun, tho' smoking in the fading west,
Again shall issue from his morning bed,
    Like a young giant vigorous from his rest.

He lives! for that is truly living when
    Our fame is a bequest from mind to mind,
His life is in the breathing hearts of men,
    Transmitted to the latest of his kind.

A Chapter from
Sketch of Handel and Beethoven - Two Lectures,
Delivered in the Lecture Hall of the Wimbledon
Village Club, Monday Evening, Dec. 14 1863;
and Monday Evening, Jan. 11, 1864

A DAY WITH
LUDWIG VON BEETHOVEN

By May Byron

At daybreak, on a summer morning, in the year 1815, a short, thick-set, sturdily-built man entered his sitting-room, and at once set to work to compose music. Not that he disturbed the slumbers of the other inhabitants by untimely noises upon the pianoforte: a course which, at three in the morning, might be resented by even the most enthusiastic admirer of his genius. No: he sat down at his table, with plenty of music paper, and addressed himself to his usual avocation of writing assiduously till noon or thereabouts.

The untidy, uncomfortable condition of his room did not distress Ludwig van Beethoven in the least. True, it was scattered all over with books and music; here the remains of last night's food, there an empty wine bottle; on the piano, the hasty sketch of some immortal work; on the floor, uncorrected proofs, business letters, orchestral scores, and MSS. in a chaotic pile.

But he thoroughly enjoyed casting a glance, from time to time, at the sunny scene without; at the vista towards the Belvedere Garden, the Danube, and the distant Carpathians,— the view for the sake of which he had taken up his lodgings at this house in the Sailer-stätte, Vienna. For if there was one thing which still could afford a unique and cloudless pleasure to this sensitive, unhappy man, it was Nature in all her varied forms of light and loveliness. Nature, that "never did betray the heart that loved her," still held out open arms of help and solace for the healing of his afflicted soul.

Beethoven, in his various migrations from lodging to lodging—and they were very numerous, and inspired by the most trivial causes—always endeavoured to select an airy, sunshiny spot, where he could at least feel the country air blowing to him, and so keep in touch with his beloved green fields. If the supply of sunshine proved insufficient, that was quite a valid reason for another removal. But his restless, sensitive mind was apt to magnify molehills into mountains, and the most trifling inconvenience into a serious obstacle to work. Work was his starting point, his course, his goal; work was his whole *raison-d'-être*, the very meaning and object of his existence.

It has been observed that if we would represent to ourselves a day in the life of Beethoven, one of the Master's own wonderful compositions would serve as the best counterpart. Wagner instances the great Quartet in C sharp minor as a notable instance of this allegoric music,—designating the rather long introductory *Adagio*, "than which, probably, nothing more melancholy has ever been expressed in tones, as the awaking of a day

'Which through its tardy course
No single longing shall fulfil—not one!'

And yet the *Adagio* is in itself a prayer, a period of conference with God, in faith, in eternal goodness." And it was in a state of mind which one may term unconsciously devotional, that the great composer now ascended into regions where few could follow him,—where, his senses deaf and blind to earthly sights and sounds, he could hold intercourse with a pure and celestial art. For Music contains, within its inexhaustible treasuries, not only all that we conceive of best, all those highest and most ennobling emotions which thrill us as at a touch of the Divine finger, but it also possesses all the characteristic beauties of other arts. The composer shares Form and Colour with the painter—a much more elastic variety of Form—and an incomparably wider use of Colour, in the magnificent paintbox of the orchestra. The composer's art, moreover, is not stationary at one fixed point—one moment, so to speak, seized and immortalised upon canvas: but has the fluidity and onward movement of actual life, passing with bewildering rapidity of transition from one phase of thought to another, even as life does. And the composer, while he shares with the great prose writer and the poet the power of expressing things marvellously well,—of uttering in beautifully poised and balanced rhythm the whole gamut of human emotion,—yet has a greater power than theirs. For he can put into a single phrase, with an exquisite intimacy of intuition, a meaning which could hardly be denoted in a hundred words: he can condense into a couple of bars the essence of a whole chapter.

The outward appearance was far from beautiful, which belied the really lofty heart of the great composer as he sat indefatigably at work. His thick, dark, upstanding hair, already turning grey, crowned a pitted, swarthy face; his looks were rugged, gloomy, forbidding; his chin bore evidence of the most superficial shaving; his hands were covered with thick black hair; his small, deeply set, fiery eyes alone redeemed him from ugliness. For the rest, he had cotton wool in his ears, and his rough, shabby, hairy clothes gave him a Crusoesque look, almost comic in its incongruity with his occupation.

The housekeeper brought in his breakfast: he paid no attention to her. He had punctiliously counted out sixty coffee-beans overnight, and handed them to her in readiness for the morning; but now, after he had dipped his pen in the coffee-cup instead of the ink some three or four times, he pushed away the discoloured mixture, and absently nibbled his crusty roll. He was composing a *Polonaise*, to be dedicated to the Empress of Russia, for which he was to receive fifty ducats. This seemed an absurdly small remuneration, but although Beethoven was "really forced" (to quote Richard Wagner) "to support himself from the proceeds of his musical labours," yet, as life had no allurements for him in the ordinary sense, he had less necessity laid on him to make much money; and "the more confident he became in the employment of his inner wealth, so much the more confidently did he make his demands outward; and he actually required from his benefactors, that they should no longer pay him for his compositions, but so provide for him that he might work altogether for himself, unconcerned as to the rest of the world. And it really happened—a thing unprecedented in the lives of musicians—that a few benevolent men of rank pledged themselves to keep Beethoven independent in the sense demanded."

So it was not with any misgivings that he set aside the score of the *Polonaise*, still unfinished, and turned to something which he justly regarded as holding promise of his best vocal work; that which is still, perhaps, the greatest love-song in the world— the unequalled *Adélaide*. Its words, though above the average of the German lyrist of that period, served merely as a peg upon which to hang the music.

> "Lonely strays thy friend in April's garden,
> Lovely fairy lights around are gleaming
> Through the tremulous boughs of rosy blossom,
>   Adélaide!
>
> In the stream, and on the snowy mountain,
> In the dying day all gold-beclouded,
> In the starry fields, thy likeness lingers,
>   Adélaide!
> Evening breezes through the leaves are lisping,
> Silver May-bells in the grasses chiming,
> Waves are rustling, nightingales are fluting—
>   Adélaide!

Soon, O wonder! on my grave a floweret,
From the ashes of my heart upspringing,
Shall reveal, on every purple petal—
    Adélaide!"

—Matthisson.

Beethoven had qualified himself for vocal writing to a degree which is rarely attempted by the instrumental composer. Although his father and grandfather had been vocalists, his own early studies had been in other branches of music; he knew little of the capabilities of the voice. So he took singing lessons from the Italian composer Salieri; and notwithstanding that his own voice was shrill and harsh, increasingly so as his deafness grew upon him, he was thus enabled to pour forth liquid and melodious phrases, such as those of *Adélaide*, which seem so absolutely adapted to the requirements of a singer that they could, so to speak, sing themselves.

"Adélaide," he said, "came entirely from my heart;" and therefore its pure ardour goes straight to the heart of the hearer. But he was not contented with his work, upon which he had already spent much time and thought. A frown gathered heavily upon his overhanging brows, as, humming the air and playing an imaginary accompaniment on the desk, he went over it again and again in the endeavour to "gild refined gold."

"The more one achieves in art," he grumbled, "the less contented is one with former works." And this, indeed, was characteristic of Ludwig van Beethoven: never to be satisfied with what he had accomplished, but to go on continually, as it were, from strength to strength. That "divine discontent which is at the root of all improvement," perpetually impelled him towards higher things, and made him at once haughtily conscious of his own powers, and yet the most modest and laborious of men.

In *Adélaide*, however, lay hidden more than the fluent

outcome of his creative instinct. It remains the lovesong for all time—the last word of a noble and ennobling passion. Here—to pursue the simile of the C sharp minor quartet—a dream-image of the *Allegro* awakened in charming reminiscence and played sweetly and sorrowfully with itself. For this rough, rugged, eccentric, bad-tempered musician was capable of reaching the austerest heights of love—those heights where renunciation sits eternally enthroned.

Love and Beethoven seem a singularly anomalous pair: yet from his youth onward love was the very mainspring of his unsullied life. It began, rooted in filial affection for his mother, of whom he wrote those touching words, "She was such a good, loving mother to me, and my best friend. Oh, no one could be more fortunate than I, when I was able to speak that sweet name 'Mother', and it was heard—and to whom shall I ever say it now?"—And it continued as a vague but fervent longing for some sweet unknown—some "not impossible She."

"Love, and love alone, is capable of bringing lasting happiness .... O God, let me find her—*her*—who will strengthen me in virtue and lawfully be mine."

So he sighed: but his hopes remained unfulfilled. "His intense longing for a home and for female companionship was never satisfied," and the extraordinary number of attachments by which his career was punctuated, and which were generally for women of superior rank to his own, were every one of them destined to be transitory and destitute of result. Magdalena Willmann, Giulietta Guicciardi, Bettine Brentano, Thérèse von Brunswick, Amalie Sebald, and many another charming phantom, passed, fugitively brilliant, across his horizon: and the domestic happiness for which Beethoven never ceased to crave, was never within measurable distance of his grasp.

But now he resolutely put away *Adélaide* and its attendant wistful thoughts, and addressed himself to more severely intellectual work: the great B flat Sonata (Op. 106) which, like all his latter work, is orchestral in feeling and treatment.

156

Beethoven was primarily and permanently a composer of sonatas; for "the great majority and most excellent of his instrumental compositions, the fundamental form of the sonata was the veil-like tissue through which he gazed into the realm of tones, or, also, through which, emerging from that realm, he made himself intelligible to us—while other forms, the mixed ones of vocal music especially, were, after all, only transitorily touched upon by him, as if by way of experiment." (Wagner.)

And one has only to reflect upon the magical and matchless beauty of his best-known work in sonata form, to be surrounded at once by a multitude of gorgeous memories. The opening movement of the "Pathétique," transfused with gloomy majesty; the *Scherzo* of the "Moonlight" Sonata, wherein a troop of glimmering fairy forms come dancing through the midnight forest: the magnificent verve and vigour of the "Waldstein;" and that unapproachable *Andante* of the "Appassionata," which some have declared they would wish to hear in dying, that the solemn glory of its pensive chords might companion them into the rest of God .... These, and innumerable other instances, each dear to the individual heart, identify Beethoven as the true lord of the Sonata.

The reader will doubtless feel some wonder that all this while the master was composing so rigorously at his desk, leaving the pianoforte untouched. But there were three very adequate reasons for this mode of action. First—that he was in the habit of writing everything, as he composed it, in notebooks; mostly out of doors in solitary rambles away from any instrument, where he would "hum to himself, and beat the air with an accompaniment of extraordinary vocal sounds." Secondly—that, being a consummate master of the science of music, and the best pianist, perhaps, of his day, he had no occasion to put to proof in actual performance, as the amateur does, the constructions of his fertile brain. Thirdly—and chiefly, and sorrowful to relate—when he had just been composing, his deafness for a while would deepen into stone-deafness: and "because of the inner world of harmony at work within his brain," said Bettine Brentano, "the external world seemed all confusion to him." Beethoven's greatest works, as years went on, were "conceived, produced and given complete to the world ... when not one of those wondrous succession of of phrases could by any possibility reach his ears:" when, in a "splendid isolation" beyond the average power to understand, he and Music dwelt alone in an inner shrine together. "Never has an earthly art created anything so serene as the symphonies in A, and F major, and all those works of the Master which date from the period of his complete deafness."

It is therefore open to doubt whether an affliction, which in an ordinary man would command our pity, was so much to be deprecated in the case of Ludwig van Beethoven as at first thoughts one might imagine. He was full of self-commiseration on its account: yet assuredly the compensations which were awarded him were such as never before fell to mortal man. By the entire exclusion of external sounds, and the entire concentration of his mind upon his work, which resulted, he was enabled to enter those unexplored altitudes whither none has followed, as none had preceded him. "He elevated music (which had been degraded, as regards its proper nature, to the rank of a merely diverting art), to the height of its sublime calling." And it must be remembered that his works were very much more remarkable, as offsprings of the early nineteenth century; than they now appear to us who are familiar with them,—to us, who are heirs of the progress of composition. For Music is the youngest of all the arts,—as compared to all others, a mere babe in arms, whose potentialities and possibilities are still but in the bud. And that Beethoven should stand where he does, on a pinnacle that none may deny, is one more proof of that isolation of genius which makes him twin with Shakespeare. These columnar intellects rise like obelisks in the midst of the ages: not to be accounted for by any rule of circumstance, or education, or heredity: and "What Beethoven's melodies produce, Shakespeare's spirit-shapes also project."

So absorbed was the master in the elaboration and evolution of his "tone-poem," that he did not see, much less hear, the timid entrance of a very shy young man. It was one Charles Neate, an English pianist, who had come, armed with a letter of introduction, to beseech the great Beethoven to receive him as a pupil for the piano.

The great Beethoven was for a moment inclined to be exceedingly bearish and inhospitable. To come on a morning when he was busy—to interrupt a man in the full flow of composition—these were unpardonable crimes! But soon his native kindliness prevailed—above all, when he discovered that his visitor was of "the noble English nation." For he held England and the English to be of an incomparable excellence: and his darling wish was to visit that favoured land, and to win a hearing there, and if possible secure an offer from some London publishing firm.

He, therefore, accepted the young man with unwonted graciousness and alacrity: looked through his compositions and gave him sound advice: and finally, thrusting away his own MSS., proposed that they two should take a little walk, to get a breath of fresh air before further operations. They passed out into the sunlit fields.

Never in all his life had Neate met a man so wholly taken up with nature, so enwrapt with the contemplation of trees, flowers, cloud, and sward. "Nature seemed his nourishment," Neate said afterwards. "He seemed to live upon and by her." The parable of the *Presto* of the C sharp minor Quartet, here was openly fulfilled,—the master, rendered, from within, completely happy, cast a glance of indescribable serenity upon the outer world. There it once more stands before him as in the Pastoral Symphony: everything is rendered luminous to him by his inner happiness.

They seated themselves upon a grassy bank, and Beethoven discoursed freely of the things dearest to his heart: his keen desire to visit England, and his fear lest his deafness might prove a hopeless obstacle to this. Neate, speaking to him in slow German, close to his left ear, managed to make himself intelligible; while the master expressed his unbounded admiration for everything English, especially Shakespeare, who was his favourite poet.

Beethoven was, indeed, as has been observed, "precisely like Shakespeare in his bearing towards the formal laws of his art, and in his emancipation from and penetration of them." He stood, as has previously been shown, nearer in point of genius to Shakespeare than to any other man: and verified the truth of Schumann's dictum that "all arts are reducible to one," and are guided by the same fundamental rules.

After a brief but exhilarating ramble in the open air, Beethoven proposed that Neate should return to dinner with him, and after that should—perhaps—receive his first lesson. The young man was overwhelmed at such unexpected kindness and *camaraderie* as he was receiving from the master, and gratefully accompanied him back to the city.

Before going to the Sailer-stätte, however, Beethoven turned into Steiner's, the music publisher's, which he was in the habit of frequenting about noon-day; where there was "nearly always a little crowd of composers, and a brisk interchange of musical opinion." (Hättenbrenner).

Beethoven was to-day in a genial and expansive frame of mind. Possibly the advent of a young Englishman had struck him as a good omen for the fulfilment of his cherished hopes towards English fame. He held forth at considerable length, upon all manner of subjects, from music to philosophy. "His criticisms were ingenuous, original, full of curious ideas" and boundless imagination. Finally, at the reiterated request of those he most favoured among the younger men, he reluctantly consented to play—to exemplify, as they cunningly put it, the opinions which he had been urging, and the laws he had been laying down.

Now, listeners on either side of a door—in or out—were, as

it has been said, Beethoven's chief aversion. Pianoforte virtuoso as he was, fine performer on the organ, violin, and viola— anything that savoured of professional display was nauseous to him. "Music the art was for him the breath of life: music the profession, as generally understood," he relegated to the depths of distaste.

He sat down with a shrug of his square shoulders, and, crooking his fingers to such a degree that his hands almost hid them, continued for a moment his tirade against the prevalent methods of playing.

"How did the old composers who were pianists, play?" he asked of his audience. "They did not run up and down the keyboard with their carefully-practised passages—*putsch, putsch, putsch!*"—and he worked the runs in a caricatured passage on the pianoforte.

"When true virtuosi played, it was comprehensive, complete.... Good, thorough work one could look into and examine.... But I pronounce judgment on no one," he added hastily, and forthwith burst into the full splendour of the *Waldstein* sonata.

His passion, his prodigious strength, amazed the Viennese, accustomed as they were to hear him, no less than the young Englishman, to whom he appeared a very prodigy of execution, as his broad, hairy, spatulate fingers, so unlike those of the typical pianist, flung themselves hither and thither upon the keys. He produced tones and effects which were hitherto undreamed of in the philosophy of the pianists of that period; and it was evident that this was no mere display of virtuosity, but that Beethoven had lost consciousness of all around him, and was simply giving vent to his own inspiration, as one possessed might do. And among the impressionable hearers, moved beyond self-control, soon not a dry eye was to be seen. Many broke into sobs; but when they would have crowded round the master, with the ultimate chord, to express in vehement gestures their boundless admiration, he rose with an almost shamefaced air, as though he had debased himself by this semi-poetic performance, and shuffled away, beckoning Neate to follow him.

The two dined alone in Beethoven's apartment in the Sailer-stätte, at his wonted time of two o'clock. The composer was not superior to creature comforts, and was very particular to have certain dishes on certain days. On Thursdays he invariably indulged in his favourite bread-soup, made with ten eggs. On Fridays he had a large haddock, with potatoes. A little Hungarian wine, or a glass of beer, sufficed him; but his favourite beverage was plenty of cold water. Water, in fact, was a necessity to him, and he rejoiced ecstatically in bathing, washing, splashing about in water; in pouring it recklessly over his hands and arms; water, internally or externally, may be said to have been his chief necessity of life.

Upon this especial occasion, the table—still littered with MSS.—was graced by Beethoven's favourite dish of macaroni and cheese, and a small dish of fish. Somewhat Spartan fare this for an Englishman; but Charles Neate was much too excited to care what he was eating.

Beethoven never composed in the afternoon, and very seldom in the evening. He had hardly sat still after dinner, smoking his long clay pipe, when—"Let us go out into the country," said he, suddenly springing up. Neate's possible piano lesson had vanished from his mind. He stuffed one or two extra note-books into his capacious pockets, and they started off—this time in a different direction.

This habit of suddenly rushing out into the open air he practised at all seasons, as the fancy took him: cold or heat, rain or sunshine, made no difference to him whatever. He had found that only among the silent solitudes of the hills and valleys could he fully release that throng of insurgent ideas which for ever clamoured in his brain for an outlet. Melodies, subjects, suggestions for their development and execution, flocked continuously through his mind; and to set them down in feverish haste—to imprison their "first fine careless rapture" in his note-book, for subsequent improvement and enlargement, was the occupation of all these country walks. But, consciously or unconsciously, his restless mind was soothed, and his sensitive nerves strengthened by the tranquil influences of the winds and skies.

Beethoven pursued his usual course on the present occasion, pulling out his note-book every few minutes, his lips moving rapidly, his eyes riveted on some mysterious distance. But he made an obvious effort at entertaining his young companion; and presently, Neate, encouraged by an unwonted stretch of conversation, or rather monologue, ventured to remark upon the master's great power in creating tone-pictures, and of the landscape-drawing, so to speak, of the Pastoral Symphony, wherein the green fields of Paradise seem to expand before earth's weary eyes, and there is

"Shed
On spirits that had long been dead,
Spirits dried up and closely furled,
The freshness of the early world."

Beethoven testified that, when composing, he always had a vision of natural beauty before his eyes, and that it enabled him to work. He had never been out of his native land: the lovely Austrian villages which he frequented, Hetzendorf, Dobling, or Heiligenstadt, sufficed him for beauty and for healthiness. But now and then, he allowed, he had a momentary longing for other scenes: the ice-blue mysteries of the Alps, or the warm and fragrant air of Italy. And he quoted—singing in a harsh, crude voice—those words of Goethe's which he had linked with such enchanting music,—the words of Mignon, yearning towards the homeland of her heart.

"Know'st thou the land, where sweet the citron blows,
Where deep in shade the golden orange glows?
A tender breeze from bluest heav'n doth stray

O'er myrtle bough and lofty laurel spray.
   Know'st thou it well? that land dost know?
O there, O there, might I with thee, Beloved, go!

Know'st thou the house, its roof on columns white?
Fair gleams the hall, the hearth is glimmering bright;
And marble statues ask, with glances mild,
'What have they done to thee? O say, poor child!'
   Know'st thou it well? that house dost know?
O there, O there, might I with thee, Beloved, go!

Know'st thou the crag, and all its cloudy grey,
Where scarce the muleteer may grope the way?
In caverns lurk the dragon's ancient brood,
Sheer falls the rock, and over it the flood.
   Know'st thou it well? the way we know—
O there, O there, my father, let us go!"

—GÖETHE,
Wilhelm Meister.

The composer at last turned homeward once more, and on arrival at his rooms, without a word of preparation, took young Neate by the shoulders and placed him upon the three-legged chair before the pianoforte. The chair promptly broke; but, nothing disconcerted, the master replaced it with another almost equally crippled, and bade the young man play.

It may be imagined with what diffidence, what nervousness, and what sinking of heart, the Englishman essayed the *Sonata Pathétique.* He paused, breathless, at the conclusion, and awaited the verdict with anxiety.

"My son," said Beethoven, clapping him on the shoulder, "you will have to play a very long time before you discover that you know nothing. But cheer up! for the young there are infinities of hope." And he proceeded, with inconceivably kind care and patience, to give the youth such teaching as he had never imagined possible. That 'bitter, sarcastic' tongue of which folk complained, that irritable temper which often alarmed the master's young lady pupils—were now conspicuously absent. For he had a peculiar sympathy with young people at the outset of their career; and no trouble was too great for him to take on their behalf.

When at length, with cordial words of encouragement, he dismissed the Englishman, Beethoven for a moment was tempted to look back upon his own early days; when, always working very hard, either as a performer or a teacher, surrounded by unloving relations and uncongenial circumstances, he struggled upward, ever upward, impelled by some irresistible wind of destiny. Then he dwelt, involuntarily, upon the gathering clouds of his manhood—the secret dread of his encroaching deafness—the hidden sorrows of unrequited love.

"Such things," he thought, "have often brought me to the border of despair, and I have come very near to putting an end to my own life. . . . Yet it seemed impossible to quit this world for ever before I had done all that I felt I was destined to accomplish . . . and how much of that is still before me! Ah! hard struggle to accomplish all which remains to be done, from the daily drudgery of necessity-work to the farthest journey, the highest flight! ... All this must be hewn out of thyself ... for thyself there is no further happiness than that which thou findest in thyself— thy art!" (*Beethoven's Diary*).

But now, with the coming of the evening hours, the composer might relax the tension of his thoughts, and find pleasure, so far as his infirmity allowed, in the society of his friends, and in talking over the newspapers. He was a well-read man, and took an eager interest in all the passing events of the day; moreover, when not in his 'serious working humour', he was a humorous, cheerful companion, full of fun and not averse from practical joking; a very different man from that 'savage personality, at loggerheads with mankind,' which he had appeared to the unsympathetic Goethe. For 'friends,' however, we had better substitute 'acquaintances'; because Beethoven declared: "I have only found two friends in the world with whom I have never had a misunderstanding. One is dead; the other still lives. Although we have heard nothing of each other for six years, I know that I still hold the place in his affections that he holds in mine."

A decided irascibility and uncertainty of temper, common to all deaf people, was apt to create rifts and coolnesses between Beethoven and those with whom he might be closely intimate. His whole warmth and abundance of affection was squandered upon his nephew Carl, the worthless son of a worthless father; an affection by no means reciprocated, which was fated only to cause fresh pangs to his much-enduring heart.

But, be that as it may, the Viennese were proud of their Beethoven—proud to be numbered among his associates. They bore him a species of personal attachment. He was part and parcel of themselves; though he moved in their midst, doubly remote from them, alike by his affliction and by his open distaste for 'the dissipations of a great and voluptuous city.' He would sit apart at a table, brooding over a long pipe and a glass of lager, his eyes half-closed; but if anyone spoke to him, or rather attempted to do so, he would always reply with ready courtesy and kindness. For, as he had written from the very depths of his heart:—

"O ye who think or say that I am rancorous, obstinate or misanthropical, what an injustice you do me! You little know the hidden cause of my appearing so. From childhood my heart and mind have been devoted to benevolent feelings, and to the thoughts of great deeds to be achieved in the future.... Born with an ardent, lively temperament, fond of social pleasures, I was early compelled to withdraw myself, and live a life of isolation from all men. At times, when I made an effort to overcome the difficulty, oh, how cruelly was I frustrated by the doubly painful experience of my defective hearing! ... Forgive me, then, if you see me turn away when I would gladly mix with you. Doubly painful is my misfortune, seeing that it is the cause of my being misunderstood. For me there can be no recreation in human intercourse, no conversation, no exchange of thoughts with my fellow-men. In solitary exile I am compelled to live."

Sometimes, however, his naturally vivacious spirits prevailed, and he became witty, satirical, 'a fellow of infinite jest.' Anything in the way of bad music was apt to send him into shouts of laughter; but "of Handel, Bach and Mozart he always spoke with the greatest reverence, and, although he would not allow his own great works to be depreciated, he himself made fun of his lesser productions. If greatly roused, he would let loose a perfect flood of hard-hitting witticisms, droll paradoxes and ideas." (*Rochlitz.*)

Still, albeit generous to a fault, and ready to give away his last thaler even to an enemy, his dislikes were so violent that he would actually take to his heels at the sight of some special object of aversion.

With particularly favoured friends, in the privacy of their own homes, Beethoven was less reticent than usual. He would discuss with them his two great regrets—that he had never visited England and had never married; which were his favourite topics of conversation. It is true that at forty-five—his present age—these regrets might still have time to be obliterated. But he felt himself the very Simeon Stylites of music, set apart to suffer in ascetic endurance upon a pillar of aloofness and despair.

And it was in this melancholy frame of mind—a reaction from the transient mirth of the evening—that the master buttoned his old grey coat about him and trudged gloomily homeward as the evening star first lighted itself. "O God, Thou lookest downward on my inward soul!" he murmured, "Thou knowest, Thou seest that love for my fellow-men, and all kindly feelings have their abode there! ... But I have no real friends; I must live alone. But I know that God is nearer to me than to many others in my art, and I commune with Him fearlessly."

Drawing a scrap of paper towards him, he scrawled a few heartfelt words upon it by the last rays of twilight:—

"I must praise Thy goodness that Thou hast left nothing undone to draw me to Thyself. It pleased Thee, early, to make me feel the heavy hand of Thy wrath, and by many chastisements to bring my proud heart low. Sickness and other misfortunes hast Thou caused to hang over me, to bring my straying from Thee to my remembrance.... But one thing I ask of Thee, my God—not to cease Thy work in my improvement ... Let me tend towards Thee, no matter by what means—and be fruitful in good works...."

And Ludwig van Beethoven had a means of "communing fearlessly" with his Creator, which, for him, was perhaps, as direct a road as prayer, if *laborare est orare*. For music, "although in its glorious fulness and power at that time unknown, was associated intimately by the early Christian writers with Christianity—with immortality." As Wagner has declared, music is of the "essential nature of things, and its kingdom is not of this world... Its spirit, like that of Christianity, is love." And by this medium, and in this divine language, the man whose outward senses were being darkened, now held, in the rapture of the "inward light," his intercourse with celestial things.

Baulked and baffled by circumstances—dragged at the chariot-wheels of relentless Fate—shut up and shut off from all sweet human amenities, the tone-artist sat down at his piano, and "after preluding softly with one hand ... poured out his soul in a very flood of harmony." At first the strains were mournful, sombre, disconnected, his own sad thoughts bearing a perpetual burden to him.

"O Providence," so he prayed, "let one more day of pure joy be vouchsafed to me! The echo of true happiness has so long been a stranger to my heart! When, when, O God! shall I again be able to feel it in the temple of nature and of man? Never? No! O, that were too hard!"

But presently he became buried in a deeper abstraction; a sphinx-like calm settled on, and smoothed out, his harsh, rough features. With the ease and firmness of a brilliant executant—with the intense feeling of an inspired artist, he continued to improvise the most glorious music which had issued that day from either his brain or his fingers. It was, like the *Allegro Finale* of the C sharp minor Quartet, "the dance of the world itself: wild delight, the lamentation of anguish, ecstasy of love, highest rapture, misery, rage, voluptuousness and sorrow." This great gift of extemporising, (which was only paralleled by his equal skill in sight-reading) was at once the solace and the snare of Beethoven. Hours upon hours could thus be dreamed away; yet who shall say that they were wasted? For gradually, out of the shifting panorama of rhythm and sound, a supreme and marvellous melody evolved itself.

For a long time—months, if not years—he had been pursuing, as it were, some beautiful, elusive phantom—the idea contained in Schiller's stirring lines commencing:—"*Freude, schöner Götterfunken*," ("*Joy, thou heavenly spark of Godhead*"). He was consumed with the desire to give these lines a worthy setting; he had filled a multitude of note-books with rough sketches; but the authentic, the indubitable melody which should be recognised at first hearing as the only one, had still evaded him until now—now, when he filled the twilight with a cry of success.

"I have it! I have it!" he exclaimed, as those magnificent phrases which were to be the crown and consummation of the great Ninth Symphony, at last were crystallised into shape upon his brain. And at that moment he entered, as it were, upon a new world of light, "in the soil of which bloomed before his sight the long-sought, divinely-sweet, innocently pure melody of humanity."

"*Joy, thou heavenly spark of Godhead!*" Was it the irony of Fate that made this thought the highest pinnacle of Beethoven's marvellous achievements? Was it not rather one of those divine compensations by which Heaven bestows, with both hands lavishly, "above all that we can desire or deserve?"

Scintillations of that "heavenly spark," multiplied a million-fold, flashed across the mental vision of the inspired composer; incessant majesties of sound piled themselves in splendid strata upon his intellectual ear; until, "blinded with excess of light," and outwearied with the exuberance of a joy beyond all that earth could yield, Ludwig van Beethoven sought his meagre straw mattress and thin quilt, and—while the clocks struck ten in the city—fell asleep as softly as a child.

FIRST PUBLISHED AS
A Day with Ludwig van Beethoven:
Days with the Great Composers, 1927

BEETHOVEN AND
HIS "IMMORTAL BELOVED"

By Gustav Kobbé

One day when Baron Spaun, an old Viennese character and a friend of Beethoven's, entered the composer's lodgings, he found the man, every line of whose face denoted, above all else, strength of character, bending over a portrait of a woman and weeping, as he muttered, "You were too good, too angelic!" A moment later, he had thrust the portrait into an old chest and, with a toss of his well-set head, was his usual self again.

As Spaun was leaving, he said to the composer, "There is nothing evil in your face to-day, old fellow."

"My good angel appeared to me this morning," was Beethoven's reply.

After the composer's death, in 1827, the portrait was found in the old chest, and also a letter, in his handwriting and evidently written to a woman, whose name, however, was not given, but who was addressed by Beethoven as his "Immortal Beloved." The letter was regarded as a great find, and biographer after biographer has stated that it must have been written to the Countess Giulietta Guicciardi, to whom he dedicated the famous "Moonlight Sonata." There was, however, one woman, who survived Beethoven more than thirty years, and who, during that weary stretch of time, knew whose was the portrait that had been found in the old chest and the identity of the woman who had returned to him the letter addressed to his "Immortal Beloved," after the strange severance of relations which both had continued to hold sacred. But she suffered in silence, and never even knew what had become of the picture.

This precious picture, which Beethoven had held in his hands and wetted with his tears, passed, with his death, into the possession of his brother Carl's widow. No one knew who it was, or took any interest in it. In 1863 a Viennese musician, Joseph Hellmesberger, succeeded in having Beethoven's remains transferred to a metallic casket, and the Beethoven family, in recognition of his efforts, made him a present of the portrait. Later it was acquired by the Beethoven Museum, in Bonn, where the master was born in 1772. There it hangs beside his own portrait, and on the back still can be read the inscription, in a feminine hand:

> "*To the rare genius, the great artist, and the good man, from T. B.*"

Who was "T. B."? If some one who had recently seen the Bonn portrait should chance to visit the National Museum in Budapest, he would come upon the bust of a woman whose features seemed familiar to him. They would grow upon him as those of the woman with the yellow shawl over her light-brown hair, a drapery of red on her shoulders and fastened at her throat, who had looked out at him from the Bonn portrait. The bust, made at a more advanced age, he would find had been placed in the museum in honor of the woman who founded the first home for friendless children in the Austrian Empire; and her name? Countess Therese Brunswick. She was Beethoven's "Immortal Beloved." "T. B."—Therese Brunswick. She was the woman who knew that the portrait found in the old chest was hers; and that the letter had been received by her shortly after her secret betrothal to Beethoven, and returned by her to him when he broke the engagement because he loved her too deeply to link her life to his.

Ludwig Van Beethoven
A Painting by Stieler

The tragedy of their romance lay in its non-fulfilment. Beethoven was a man of noble nature, yet what had he to offer her in return for her love? His own love, it is true. But he was uncouth, stricken with deafness, and had many of the "bad moments" of genius. He foresaw unhappiness for both, and, to spare her, took upon himself the great act of renunciation. We

173

need only recall him weeping over the picture of his Therese. And Therese? To her dying day she treasured his memory. Very few shared her secret. Her brother Franz, Beethoven's intimate friend, knew it. Baron Spaun also divined the cause of his melancholy. Some years after the composer's death, Countess Therese Brunswick conceived a great liking for a young girl, Miriam Tenger, whom she had taken under her care for a short period, until a suitable school was selected for her in Vienna. When the time for parting came, Miriam burst into tears and clung to the Countess's hand.

"Child! Child!" exclaimed the lady, "do you really love me so deeply?"

"I love you, I love you so," sobbed the child, "that I could die for you."

The Countess placed her hand on the girl's head. "My child," she said, "when you have grown older and wiser, you will understand what I mean when I say that to *live* for those we love shows a far greater love, because it requires so much more courage. But while you are in Vienna, there is one favor you can do me, which my heart will consider a great one. On the twenty-seventh of every March go to the Wahringer Cemetery and lay a wreath of immortelles on Beethoven's grave."

When, true to her promise, the girl went with her school principal to the cemetery, they found a man bending over the grave and placing flowers upon it. He looked up as they approached.

"The child comes at the request of the Countess Therese Brunswick," explained the principal.

"The Countess Therese Brunswick! Immortelles upon this grave are fit from her alone." The speaker was Beethoven's faithful friend, Baron Spaun.

In 1860, when the leaves of thirty-three autumns had fallen upon the composer's grave and the Countess had gone to her last resting-place, a voice, like an echo from a dead past, linked the names of Beethoven and the woman he had loved. There was at that time in Germany a virtuosa, Frau Hebenstreit, who when a young girl had been a pupil of Beethoven's friend, the violinist Schuppanzigh. At a musical, in the year mentioned, she had just taken part in a performance of the third "Leonore" overture, when, as if moved to speak by the beauty of the music, she suddenly said: "Only think of it! Just as a person sits to a painter for a portrait, Countess Therese Brunswick was the model for Beethoven's Leonore. What a debt the world owes her for it!" After a pause she went on:

"Beethoven never would have dared marry without money, and a countess, too—and so refined, and delicate enough to blow away. And he—an angel and a demon in one! What would have become of them both, and of his genius with him?" So far as I have been able to discover, this was the first even semi-public linking of the two names.

Yet all these years there was one person who knew the secret—the woman who as a school-girl had placed the wreath of immortelles on Beethoven's grave for her much-loved Countess Therese Brunswick. Through this act of devotion Miriam Tenger seemed to become to the Countess a tie that stretched back to her past, and though they saw each other only at long intervals, Miriam's presence awakened anew the old memories in the Countess's heart, and from her she heard piecemeal, and with pauses of years between, the story of hers and Beethoven's romance.

Therese was the daughter of a noble house. Beethoven was welcome both as teacher and guest in the most aristocratic circles of Vienna. The noble men and women who figure in the dedications of his works were friends, not merely patrons. Despite his uncouth manners and appearance, his genius, up to the point at least when it took its highest flights in the "Ninth Symphony" and the last quartets, was appreciated; and he was a figure in Viennese society. The Brunswick house was one of many that were open to him. The Brunswicks were art lovers. Franz, the son of the house, was the composer's intimate friend.

The mother had all possible graciousness and charm, but with it also a passionate pride in her family and her rank, a hauteur that would have caused her to regard an alliance between Therese and Beethoven as monstrous. Therese was an exceptional woman. She had an oval, classic face, a lovely disposition, a pure heart and a finely cultivated mind. The German painter, Peter Cornelius, said of her that any one who spoke with her felt elevated and ennobled. The family was of the right mettle. The Countess Blanka Teleki, who was condemned to death for complicity in the Hungarian uprising of 1848, but whose sentence was commuted to life imprisonment—she finally was released in 1858,—was Therese's niece, and is said to have borne a striking likeness to her. It may be mentioned that Giulietta Guicciardi, of the "Moonlight Sonata," was Therese's cousin. There seems no doubt that the composer was attracted to Giulietta before he fell in love with his "Immortal Beloved." That is why his biographers were so ready to believe that the letter was addressed to the lady with the romantic name and identified with one of his most romantic works.

Therese herself told Miriam that one day Giulietta, who had become the affianced of Count Gallenberg, rushed into her room, threw herself at her feet like a "stage princess," and cried out: "Counsel me, cold, wise one! I long to give Gallenberg his congé and marry the wonderfully ugly, beautiful Beethoven, if—if only it did not involve lowering myself socially." Therese, who worshipped the composer's genius and already loved him secretly, turned the subject off, fearful lest she should say, in her indignation at the young woman who thought she would be lowering herself by marrying Beethoven, something that might lead to an irreparable breach. "Moonlight Sonata," or no "Moonlight Sonata," there are two greater works by the same genius that bear the Brunswick name,—the "Appassionata," dedicated to Count Franz Brunswick, and the sonata in F-sharp major, Opus 78, dedicated to Therese, and far worthier of her chaste beauty and intellect than the "Moonlight."

It will be noticed that Giulietta called Therese the "cold, wise one." Her purity led her own mother to speak other as an "anchoress." Yet it was she who from the time she was fifteen years old to the day of her death cherished the great composer in her heart; and of her love for him were the mementos that he sacredly guarded. When Therese was fifteen years old she became Beethoven's pupil. The lessons were severe. Yet beneath the rough exterior she recognized the heart of a nobleman. The "cold, wise one," the "anchoress," fell in love with him soon after the lessons began, but carefully hid her feelings from every one. There is a charming anecdote of the early acquaintance of the composer and Therese.

The children of the house of Brunswick were carefully brought up. During the music lessons the mother was accustomed to sit in an adjoining room with the door between open. One bitterly cold winter day Beethoven arrived at the appointed hour. Therese had practised diligently, but the work was difficult and, in addition, she was nervous. As a result she began too fast, became disconcerted when Beethoven gruffly called out "*Tempo!*" and made mistake after mistake, until the master, irritated beyond endurance, rushed from the room and the house in such a hurry that he forgot his overcoat and muffler. In a moment Therese had picked up these, reached the door and was out in the street with them, when the butler overtook her, relieved her of them and hurried after the composer's retreating figure.

When the girl entered the doorway again, she came face to face with her mother, who, fortunately, had not seen her in the street, but who was scandalized that a daughter of the house of Brunswick should so far have forgotten herself and her dignity as to have run after a man even if only to the front door, and with his overcoat and muffler. "He might have caught cold and died," gasped Therese, in answer to her mother's remonstrance. What would the mother have said had she known that her daughter actually had run out into the street, and had been prevented from following Beethoven until she overtook him only by the butler's timely action!

Therese's brother Franz was devoted to her. As a boy he had taken his other sister (afterward Blanka Teleki's mother) out in a boat on the "Mediterranean," one of the ponds at Montonvasar, the Brunswick country estate. The boat upset. Therese, who was watching them from the bank, rushed in and hauled them out. Franz was asked if he had been frightened. "No," he answered, "I saw my good angel coming."

When he became intimate with Beethoven, he told the composer about this incident, and also how, after that stormy music lesson, Therese had started to overtake him with his coat and muffler. Knowing what a lonely, unhappy existence the composer led, he could not help adding that life would be very different if he had a good angel to watch over him, such as he had in his sister.

Franz little knew that his words fell upon Beethoven like seed on eager soil. From that time on he looked at Therese with different eyes. His own love soon taught him to know that he was loved in return. No pledge had yet passed between them when, in May, 1806, he went to Montonvasar on a visit; but one evening there, when Therese was standing at the piano listening to him play, he softly intoned Bach's—

> "Would you your true heart show me,
>   Begin it secretly,
> For all the love you trow me,
>   Let none the wiser be.
> Our love, great beyond measure,
>   To none must we impart;
> So, lock our rarest treasure
>   Securely in your heart."

"Beethoven at Heiligenstadt"
A Painting by Carl Schmidt

Next morning they met in the park. He told her that at last he had discovered in her the model for his Leonore, the heroine of his opera "Fidelio." "And so we found each other"—these were the simple words with which, many years later, Therese concluded the narrative of her betrothal with Beethoven to Miriam Tenger.

The engagement had to be kept a secret. Had it become known, it would have ended in his immediate dismissal by the Countess' mother. In only one person was confidence reposed, Franz, the devoted brother and treasured friend. Therese's income was small, and Franz, knowing the opposition with which the proposed match would meet, pointed out to Beethoven that it would be necessary for him to secure a settled position and income before the engagement could be published and the marriage take place. The composer himself saw the justice of this, and assented.

Early in July Beethoven left Montonvasar for Furen, a health resort on the Plattensee, which he reached after a hard trip. Fatigued, grieving over the first parting from Therese, and downcast over his uncertain future, he there wrote the letter to his "Immortal Beloved," which is now one of the treasures of the Berlin Library. It is a long letter, much too long to be given here in full, written for the most part in ejaculatory phrases, and curiously alternating between love, despair, courage and hopefulness and commonplace, everyday affairs. Nor will space permit me to tell how Alexander W. Thayer, an American, who spent a great part of his life and means in gathering detailed and authentic data for a Beethoven biography,—which, however, he did not live to finish,—worked out the year in which this letter was written (Beethoven gave only the day of the month); showed that it must be 1806; proved further that it could not have been intended for Giulietta Guicciardi, yet did not venture to state that Countess Therese Brunswick was the undoubted recipient. Afterward, I believe, he heard of Miriam Tenger, entered into correspondence with her, and the letters doubtless will be found among his papers; but he did not live to make use of the information.

One of the reasons why the identity of the recipient of Beethoven's letter remained so long unknown was that he did not address her by name. The letter begins: "My angel, my all, myself!" In order to secure a fixed position, Beethoven had decided to try Prussia and even England, and this intention he refers to when, after apostrophizing Therese as his "immortal beloved," he writes these burning words:

"Yes, I have decided to toss abroad so long, until I can fly to your arms and call myself at home with you, and let my soul, enveloped in your love, wander through the kingdom of spirits." The letter has this exclamatory postscript:

"Eternally yours!
Eternally mine!
Eternally one another's!"

The engagement lasted until 1810, four years, when the letters, which through Franz's aid had passed between Beethoven and Therese, were returned. Therese, however, always treasured as one of her "jewels" a sprig of immortelle fastened with a ribbon to a bit of paper, the ribbon fading with passing years, the paper growing yellow, but still showing the words: "*L'Immortelle à son Immortelle—Luigi.*"

It had been Beethoven's custom to enclose a sprig of immortelle in nearly every letter he sent her, and all these sprigs she kept in her desk many, many years. She made a white silken pillow of the flowers; and, when death came at last, she was laid at rest, her head cushioned on the mementos of the man she had loved.

A Chapter from
The Loves of Great Composers, 1905

Made in the USA
Las Vegas, NV
25 April 2023

71069133R00111